From Head to Toe

Bound Feet, Bathing Suits, and Other Bizarre and Beautiful Things

JANICE WEAVER

Illustrations by Francis Blake

Tundra Books

For David, with love always

Text copyright © 2003 by Janice Weaver
Illustrations copyright © 2003 by Francis Blake

Published in Canada by Tundra Books,
481 University Avenue, Toronto, Ontario M5G 2E9

Published in the United States by Tundra Books of Northern New York,
P.O. Box 1030, Plattsburgh, New York 12901

Library of Congress Control Number: 2003106861

National Library of Canada Cataloguing in Publication

Weaver, Janice
From head to toe : bound feet, bathing suits, and other
bizarre and beautiful things / Janice Weaver; illustrated by Francis Blake.

Includes index.

ISBN 0-88776-654-4

1. Clothing and dress – History – Juvenile literature. 2. Fashion – History – Juvenile literature. I. Blake,
Francis II. Title.

GT518.W43 2003   j391   C2003-903049-0

We acknowledge the financial support of the Government of Canada through the Book Publishing Industry Development Program (BPIDP) and that of the Government of Ontario through the Ontario Media Development Corporation's Ontario Book Initiative. We further acknowledge the support of the Canada Council for the Arts and the Ontario Arts Council for our publishing program.

Design: Terri Nimmo

Printed and bound in Canada

2 3 4 5 6   08 07 06 05 04

Contents

Acknowledgments

THIS BOOK DID NOT COME EASILY, but it would not have come at all without the help of friends, family, and colleagues. I must thank, in particular, my wonderful parents and first readers, Robert and Audrey Weaver; my many close friends, especially Mark Bell, Alison Reid, and Caryl Silver; and my astute editor, Kathryn Cole. The people at Tundra Books – Jenny Bradshaw, Catherine Mitchell, Alison Morgan, Kong Njo, Melanie Storoschuk, Tamara Sztainbok, and Sue Tate – have been more helpful and patient than I had any right to expect. I reserve a special thanks for my publisher, Kathy Lowinger, who greeted this idea with her trademark enthusiasm and kept up her excitement from beginning to end. Terri Nimmo is a talented designer who has become a good friend, and this book certainly would not have been the same without her.

I was helped in the writing of this project by some grants through the Ontario Arts Council's Writers' Reserve Program, and I would like to acknowledge the support of the OAC and of the publisher-recommenders, especially Don Bastian of the sadly now-defunct Stoddart Publishing and Sheba Meland and Anne Shone of Maple Tree Press.

Last but far from least, I must thank Francis Blake. I had a picture of this book in my head, and when I first saw samples of Francis's artwork, I knew he was the man for the job. Despite challenges of both time and distance, he came through with illustrations that add so much to the overall look and humor of the book. If I had to be upstaged, I'm glad he was the one to do it.

The Naked Truth

WE HAVE BEEN USING OUR CLOTHES – and even our own skin and hair – to express ourselves as long as we have been walking this earth. Early people smeared their skin with plant dyes, draped their necks with shells and feathers, and styled their hair with mud. Today, having evolved so much from our prehistoric ancestors, we smear our skin with makeup, drape our necks with gold and silver, and style our hair with mousse and hairspray.

The clothes we wear, the makeup we put on, and the hairstyles we choose to sport undeniably say a lot about who we are and what we believe. But they also reflect the times we live in. They are like a kind of a visual language, one full of information about cultural traditions, local customs and superstitions, gender roles, social status, and political convictions. They have separated rich from poor, widened the gap between women and men, sparked riotous behavior in otherwise ordinary people, and launched wars that dragged on for centuries. They have even entered our everyday speech, giving us words and phrases that we continue to use long after the items that inspired them have been forgotten.

This book travels across thousands of years and through countless cultures and countries to tell the story of fashion in some of its weirdest, wildest, and most wonderful forms. It's not a history of fashion, in the strictest sense of the word, but is more of a whirlwind tour of a few of the more outlandish things we've done in our quest to stand out or our desire to blend in. It asks why we wear what we wear, and it shows how the trends we follow echo the greater social and cultural changes of our times. In the end, we're left with a picture not so much of what we wear but of who we are.

Girl Power

if you'd been a woman in the mid-1800s, you would have spent your days lugging around skirts that were often as wide as you were tall, in corsets that forced you to keep your breathing shallow. And forget about wearing comfortable shoes or showing your legs in public – such things were unthinkable. In those days, women were genuinely believed to be weaker and more vulnerable, and many men (and more than a few women too!) thought that things like politics, business, and physical activity could be dangerous for them – perhaps even fatal. Women's clothes reflected these beliefs. They were designed to make it difficult for those who wore them to be active and involved.

But in the mid-1800s, life slowly began to improve for women. Society was changing, and new inventions such as the typewriter and the telephone were making it possible for them to become busier and less isolated. One crucial invention, surprisingly enough, was the bicycle. Mass-produced and inexpensive to buy, the bicycle was readily available to people of all social classes, male and female, and it was a huge factor in releasing women from the sheltered, inactive lives they had been leading.

Of course, no woman in her right mind was going to hop on a bicycle when she had to lug around fifteen pounds (7 kilograms) or more of skirts and petticoats. And that was where Amelia Bloomer entered the picture. This early American suffragette (women's rights activist) published *The Lily*, the first newspaper written and edited entirely by women. Bloomer argued for many new roles for women, and she spent a lot of time condemning what she believed were the ridiculous and restrictive clothes they were made to wear. She was so vocal in her support of a type of loose-fitting, practical trouser, in fact, that the pants – bloomers – still bear her name today.

Modern women can pretty much wear whatever they want, but that wasn't the case for Amelia Bloomer and others who wanted to spark a revolution in women's fashion. These so-called Bloomer Girls, tooling around town on their bicycles, looked carefree

and untroubled, but often they were the subject of ridicule and sometimes were even pelted with stones as they passed. Elizabeth Smith Miller, who actually invented the bloomer pants, reported enduring "much gaping curiosity and the harmless jeering of street boys." Many thought these women were trying to behave too much like men, and they worried what would happen if they were allowed to continue challenging common beliefs. Would women next want the right to vote? Would they want to own businesses and become doctors and lawyers? Would they begin to think they could have a life outside the home if that's what they chose?

Skirting the issue

Most of Bloomer's frustration was focused on a particularly cumbersome article of clothing known as the hoop skirt. Introduced in 1856, this underskirt was actually hailed as a huge leap forward for women because it freed them from having to wear heavy horsehair or stiffened linen crinolines to hold out their skirts in the fashionable bell shape of the time. Also called the cage crinoline, the hoop skirt was a series of progressively larger steel rings attached to strips of cloth tape. It's hard to imagine today that this represented any kind of advancement for women, but in fact the rings were considerably lighter and cooler to wear than an ordinary crinoline.

Unfortunately, whatever advantages the hoop skirt may initially have offered were quickly lost. Spurred on by the possibilities of these "liberating" new garments, manufacturers began making the hoops bigger and bigger. By the early 1860s, women's skirts were routinely five or more feet (1.5 meters) wide. This gave rise to a whole new set of challenges. It was almost impossible for a woman dressed this way to get into a public carriage without male assistance, for instance, and once inside, most women had to kneel on the floor because the hoops would flip the skirt up in a revealing manner. Some chose the more scandalous option of removing their hoop skirts altogether (leaving on their overskirts, of course) so they could get on and off these early buses with relative ease. It was not unusual to see such carriages trundling down the streets with several hoop skirts hanging off the sides.

The hoop skirt was really just a new spin on an old idea – sixteenth- and seventeenth-century women had a version of it in an underskirt known as the farthingale. Supposedly first invented in the late 1400s by a Portuguese queen who needed to mask a difficult-to-explain pregnancy, the farthingale was a linen petticoat reinforced with hoops of whalebone or steel. Like the hoop skirt, it flared out to absurd dimensions, making it difficult for women to maneuver. Many farthingale devotees took to kneeling on cushions strewn about the floor because the act of sitting in a chair simply became too difficult to manage. Of course, that level of inconvenience wasn't available to just anyone; the widest farthingales were restricted by law to the highest members of society.

In France, the farthingale was rejected in favor of the *bourrelet*, or, more baldly stated, the bum roll. As its name suggests, this was a roll of felt padding that was stuffed around the waist and the derriere to create the same effect as the farthingale. The wearer's overskirts would flare out over this roll and then gently drape down in the shape of a bell.

By the eighteenth century, the bum roll had transformed itself into

9

something even more ridiculous – the pannier skirt. It was made up of two separate wire-and-cloth baskets that hung from the hips just like the panniers that cyclists hook to the sides of their bikes today. Taking their name from the wicker carrying baskets that were often hung from donkeys and other work animals, these eighteenth-century panniers were usually made of wood or whalebone and were designed to extend women's skirts at the sides but not in front or behind.

As the popularity of the pannier grew, so too did its breadth. By the mid-1700s, women's skirts sometimes jutted out to as much as eight feet (more than 2 meters). Chairs had to have their armrests removed, and many women could not make it through doorways without turning sideways – and some not even then! At a performance of Handel's *Messiah* in Dublin, pannier lovers were reportedly implored to leave the contraptions at home so the theater could accommodate

seven hundred people instead of six hundred. And still women of style struggled on, until at last someone came up with the idea of a collapsible pannier that could be folded away when the need arose.

In light of all this, perhaps it's not surprising that many women cheered the arrival of the hoop skirt in the 1850s. If those same women had been able to peer ahead another hundred years or so, they would no doubt have been shocked by what they saw: miniskirts and micro-minis that left so little to the imagination, they made the days when women feared exposing an ankle to the gaze of a man seem remarkably oppressive.

The Sock Market

When hemlines first began their slow climb to mid-thigh, women found they had a lot more to worry about than that inadvertent flash of ankle. They suddenly had to start paying attention to a lengthy expanse they had mostly been able to ignore before: their legs. Knowing that men – and even other women – would be taking a good, long look at what had, for centuries,

MARY, MARY QUANT CONTRARY

Often called the "mother of the miniskirt," Mary Quant was a London-based designer who spearheaded the 1960s fashion revolution. She believed in creating clothes that were affordable and challenged convention – sometimes to an extreme degree. "Good taste is death," she once proclaimed. "Vulgarity is life."

From her shop in a trendy area of London known as Chelsea, Quant sold clothes of her own design in numbers that astonished even her. The miniskirt and micro-mini were her most famous creations, but she's also associated with plastic raincoats, paintbox make-up, and the ever-popular hot pants.

Quant's design philosophy was based in a strongly held belief that fashion should be for everyone, not just the privileged few. She wanted to take the snobbery out of fashion, she said, so she mass-produced her clothes to keep the prices down.

While her styles weren't for everyone, they were a much-needed departure from the conservative skirt-and-sweater sets of the 1950s and early 1960s. Quant believed a designer should be giving people what they want before they even know they want it. "Fashion doesn't really influence the climate of opinion," she once remarked, "it reflects what people are reading and thinking and listening to."

remained hidden from view, most women wanted to make their legs look their best. To give them a nice, even tone and mask any blemishes or imperfections, they turned to stockings.

Stockings are actually an ancient article of clothing. They were first worn as early as 400 B.C. for both warmth and comfort – by men. We associate men in stockings mostly with the late 1400s and 1500s, however, when no self-respecting nobleman would be caught without his hose. In 1589, with the advent of a machine that could knit stockings, men of all classes started slipping them on.

Of course, women wore them too. Though rarely seen under everything else they had to wear, thick wool or cotton stockings were the norm until around the end of the First World War, when a finer version was developed. Although they were similar to what we today call nylons or pantyhose, these stockings came in individual pieces – that is, one for each leg – and they were held up with garters and came in different sizes, just like shoes. They were usually made of silk, which was luxurious and pleasant to wear (hence the term "silky smooth") but also snagged easily and was too expensive for many average women to afford. Stocking-wearers everywhere were delighted when a chemist named Wallace Carothers began a series of experiments that led to the development of nylon in 1939. This synthetic fabric was much cheaper to buy, so women didn't have to worry quite as much about laddering, or putting a run in, their stockings.

The introduction of nylon to the consumer market was delayed by the Second World War. All the nylon that could be produced was needed by the military for tents, belts, and especially parachutes. Some already-made nylon stockings were reportedly collected and melted down to be turned into tires for the army. But eventually the material found its way back into the marketplace. On the first day nylon stockings appeared in New York, more than three-quarters of a million pairs were sold!

Nylons were originally made much like any other type of clothing – they were sewn flat and then joined with a seam. Women would wear the seam at the backs of their legs, and care was taken to ensure that it always remained straight. Crooked seams were the sign of a slovenly dresser, and some women took great pride in their ability to keep

them in line. With the shortage of stockings during the war, many even drew fake seams up their legs with makeup (or had friends do it for them, more likely). Then the challenge became to sit down on a bus or in a chair without accidentally rubbing the seam away.

In the 1960s, hosiery manufacturers developed a way of knitting nylons in the shape of a tube, making the seams a thing of the past. This was welcome news for most women, who never quite got the knack of keeping theirs straight. But those who had become accomplished at it, and thought the skill spoke to their elegance and sophistication, were sorry to see them go. These same

women were due for another shock: by the mid-1960s, the miniskirt had climbed so far up the thigh that garters were also eliminated. That's when manufacturers started to make combined hose and panties – or pantyhose.

Waist Reduction

For many modern women, pantyhose are the bane of their existence. They sag and run and creep ever downward over the course of the day. They make the legs much too hot in the summer and offer little protection from cold winds in the winter. But those who are

THE MORE THINGS CHANGE . . .

If you think the days of the corset and its accompanying medical problems are long behind us, think again. Doctors have recently determined that a condition known as *meralgia paresthetica* — to the rest of us, a tingling or burning sensation in the thighs — can be caused by too-tight low-rise jeans.

It seems the offending denims, preferred by girls modest in both age and waist size, are pinching a nerve found just below the hip bone. This nerve supplies the front part of the thigh, and compressing it can result in not only that tingling sensation but also heightened sensitivity or numbness in the area. This isn't too far removed, perhaps, from the corset's reign of terror on Victorian women's circulatory systems and digestive tracts.

Still, afflicted girls don't need to panic. There is a simple, foolproof cure: turn those hip-huggers in for a pair of looser-fitting pants!

tempted to complain about the price fashion demands should realize that things could be – and have been – much, much worse.

The torturous corset was introduced in the 1500s, though women had been binding themselves up with strips of fabric since ancient times. Wall paintings from Greece and Rome show women with their breasts bound or their stomachs cinched in bodices, in what was probably an early form of underwear. The sixteenth-century corset was a much more complicated apparatus, most often made of leather, or occasionally canvas; the stays, or rigid supports, were generally metal, horn, or whalebone. The massive demand for corsets was even partly responsible for the explosive growth of the whaling industry.

Traditionally, corsets came in many different styles and sizes. They could be lightly or heavily boned, and would lace up to anywhere from more than thirty inches (75 centimeters) to less than eighteen (45 centimeters). There were also special corsets for pregnant women, men, and even children.

The most tightly laced corsets, which were at the height of their popularity in the 1800s, could reduce a woman's waist measurement by as much as ten inches (25 centimeters). The practice of tight-lacing was so extreme, in fact, that the wearer's ribs would sometimes overlap and her internal organs could be crushed. Her ability to breathe was certainly compromised – hence the popularity of the strategically placed Victorian fainting couch.

There's no question that cinching in the waist by several inches could create physical complications. But corsets were accused of causing or intensifying all manner of problems – from spinal deformities to some cancers to wild, immoral behavior – that they really had no hand in. One commonly held belief was that corsets affected the flow of blood – either by directing it away from women's reproductive organs (where blood was needed for good child-bearing) or by directing it to the brain (where it could do no good at all).

Like so many other items of clothing, corsets were a symbol of status and affluence. They were adopted first by noblewomen, who wore them as proof of their restraint and good breeding. When the Industrial Revolution of the early 1800s made corsets more plentiful and less expensive, they found their way into the wardrobes of working women. Nevertheless, the corset remained a sign of refinement; women who dared go without – like Amelia Bloomer – were often denounced as lazy and even promiscuous.

The battle to rid the world of corsets was hard-fought and lengthy. Suffragettes began railing against the contraptions in the mid-1800s, but many women continued to wear them into the middle decades of the twentieth century. Once again, war played a

part in changing fashion. In 1917, some American women were able to breathe a little easier – literally and figuratively – having donated their corsets to the war effort. Once melted down, the reclaimed stays reportedly produced enough metal to build two battleships!

But what really spelled the end for the corset was the advent of the less restrictive girdle, around the 1920s, and the invention of flexible, stretchable Lycra, in 1960. The life of the girdle was short lived, however; in the bra-burning days of the 1970s, women wanted to be free and natural, not squeezed into garments that seemed the very symbols of more restrictive times. Today, most fashion historians agree, women have essentially internalized the corset through diet, exercise, and even plastic surgery. In the new millennium, the quest to reshape our bodies has moved from the outside in.

Bathing Beauties

When women finally freed themselves once and for all from the tyranny of the corset, they began to see the possibilities in leading truly unencumbered lives. It was around this same time that the bathing suit really came into its own.

For centuries, the idea of bathing for sport or pleasure – instead of just for therapeutic or hygienic reasons – was lost. We know the ancient Greeks and Romans did it, but somewhere along the way, the custom disappeared. Spas and public bathhouses didn't resurface in Europe until the 1700s, and swimming as a recreational activity was another 150 years behind that.

The Industrial Revolution helped Europeans and North Americans rediscover the pleasures of the sea. Railroads began to appear in the 1820s and 1830s, and this made seaside weekends and holidays possible. There also slowly emerged the idea of regulated workweeks, with evenings and weekends off. People began looking for activities to fill what came to be called their leisure time.

The typical Victorian beach scene was certainly nothing like what you would see today, however. People went to great lengths to protect their skin from the sun – not out of fear of UV rays, like modern sun worshippers, but because tanned skin told the world that you worked outdoors and thus were of a lower class. Women and men bathed separately, and it was common

for women to use bathing machines, which were like little portable cabanas. These would be wheeled by horses into the water, where the truly daring could venture out to splash around without fear of being spotted by lustful men. Any who did get a peek would have been thoroughly disappointed – the typical lady's bathing costume of the early 1800s included long sleeves, a smock that reached to the ankles, and often a bonnet and a shawl.

By the 1860s, the influence of Amelia Bloomer was beginning to be felt even on the beaches of America.

Women started to wear bloomer pants – of flannel or wool! – as part of their swimming costume. These were topped with knee-length dresses and finished off with fashionable black wool stockings, bathing slippers, and ruffled caps. All this heavy fabric made it virtually impossible for women to do much more than splash about briefly in the water and return to the privacy of their bathing machines. They didn't take up swimming as an actual sport until the first decades of the twentieth century.

In the 1920s, there was a seismic shift in the way Europeans and North

Americans viewed the sun. With most working people now stuck indoors all day in factories and offices, white, untanned skin was no longer taken as a sign of wealth and privilege. In fact, the pendulum swung fully to the other side, and those who were rich enough to afford not to work began sunning themselves on the sandy shores of the world's seaside resorts. When the fashion designer Coco Chanel was photographed flashing her dark, sun-kissed skin, the trend was officially launched. Everyone who was anyone went in search of the perfect tan.

Of course, it's impossible to acquire that perfect tan if you're covered from neck to wrist to ankle, so soon the wool stockings and bloomers of the past several decades were being cast off in favor of one-piece bathing suits in stretchable fabrics. Not everyone took to these suits like fish to the ocean, however; when a well-known Australian swimmer named Annette Kellerman appeared on a Massachusetts beach sporting the new look in 1907, she was promptly arrested for indecent exposure.

By the time the twentieth century had reached its midpoint, many people were looking back at Kellerman and others like her as the very models of virtue and modest dress. One-piece suits seemed to cost more and be made with less fabric with each passing year. And in 1946, the world was really turned on its head when the French designer Louis Reard unveiled his latest creation, the bikini, which he claimed revealed everything about its wearer "except her mother's maiden name." This skimpy two-piece suit was named for the islands of the Bikini Atoll, in the Pacific Ocean, where the United States tested an atomic bomb that same year. It's hard to say which event had a more explosive impact on society.

The road from tight-laced corsets to string bikinis and beyond has been long, meandering, and filled with bumps and potholes. But as far as fashion has traveled, women themselves have traveled even farther. Just as those early opponents of Amelia Bloomer feared, they did want the right to vote, the opportunity to own businesses and become working professionals, and the freedom to have a life outside the home. For many women, clothes were the sites of the first skirmishes in a long war to be regarded as equal citizens. One hundred and fifty years later, the battle rages on.

Clothes Make the Man

In the early 1940s, war in Europe was a huge global concern. Even in North America, many cities were on the verge of chaos. Men were away fighting and dying overseas, rationing of food and clothing was in effect, and fear was running high. In Los Angeles, thousands of Japanese Americans had been deported from a neighborhood known as Little Tokyo and shipped to prison camps where they would wait out the war. Thousands more Hispanics from Mexico and elsewhere in the United States were arriving in the city every month in search of work as farm laborers. The face of Los Angeles was changing, and in those days of great anxiety and suspicion, anyone who was viewed as "non-American" seemed like a potential threat. Adding to the tension was the fact that the city was also a waystation for many soldiers and sailors on their way to war. Pumped up by their basic training and nervous about what lay ahead, these men were too often searching for an easy way to let off steam.

When a young Hispanic farmhand was killed in an incident that came to be known as the Sleepy Lagoon Murder, many servicemen found the excuse they had been looking for. Newspapers stirred the pot by printing stories about violent Mexican gangs running rampant through the streets, and soon most white Angelenos were convinced that Hispanics were a threat that had to be dealt with. The arrest and subsequent murder trial of seventeen young men just cemented that belief.

Throughout May and early June of 1943, sailors and soldiers clashed daily with groups of young Hispanic men in what the newspapers dubbed the Zoot Suit Riots. The Hispanics, known as *pachucos*, or punks, were mad about these suits, which featured long jackets that reached to the knees and had broad shoulders and wide lapels. The pants rode high on the waist, ballooned out at the knee, and then tapered back down at the cuff. Huge hats with oversized brims and watch chains that dangled from waist to mid-calf completed the look. In a time of hardship – when the U.S. government had ordered that men's suits be made without cuffs, pleats, or patch pockets to save on fabric – people viewed the zoot suiters' extravagance as an insult to the war effort, and even as disrespectful to those who had lost their lives. Angry gangs of white servicemen and other self-appointed "good" citizens began to roam the Hispanic neighborhoods, looking for zoot suiters. When they found one, they would drag him to the middle of the street, cut his long hair, strip him, and set his clothes on fire. The message to other zoot suiters was clear: if you buck the system, you'll pay the price.

The Zoot Suit Riots proved how easy it is for fashion to become bound up with all kinds of complicated social and moral issues. The riots were about patriotism, freedom of expression, social status, and especially race. The zoot suiters had made it clear they weren't going to be told where they could go, what jobs they could hold, or what clothes they could wear. They were North America's first rebellious teenagers.

Smells like Teen Spirit

The Zoot Suit Riots were finally put down in a remarkably ordinary way: the Los Angeles city council passed a resolution banning the suits on local streets. Today we may view this as an extraordinary infringement of freedom of expression, but in fact the councilors of Los Angeles – whether they knew it or not – were really just enacting a sumptuary law, a type of ruling that kings and politicians had been using for centuries to regulate what people wore and how and where they could wear it. In Los Angeles, anyone who violated the resolution against zoot suits faced thirty days in jail, so not surprisingly, offenders were few and far between. Still, no mere local bylaw could quash the spirit of teenage rebellion the Zoot Suit Riots had awakened.

The successors of the zoot suiters were the beatniks of the 1950s, the hippies of the 1960s, and every angry, disillusioned teenager ever since. But while this defiant new attitude survived, the zoot suit itself did not. In no time, it had been replaced by an item of clothing that has been part of the uniform of rebellious teenagers from that day to this one: blue jeans.

Many people believe the inventor of blue jeans was a German American named Levi Strauss. In 1853, Strauss set out for the rough-and-tumble frontier town of San Francisco to make his fortune selling supplies to miners seeking their own fortunes in the California gold rush. Strauss sold bedding, undergarments, and all kinds of other clothing, including some tough, durable pants made out of a material called denim (probably from the French phrase *serge de Nimes*, which was used to describe a fabric made in southern France since at least the 1600s).

There is a romantic story that has Strauss making a pair of pants out of tent canvas and dying them blue for a customer who wants trousers that won't rip and won't show the dirt. This is probably why he is remembered today as the pants' inventor, but unfortunately, the story is most likely not true. In the great San Francisco earthquake of 1906, all of the records of Levi Strauss & Co. were destroyed, erasing the early part of the company's history and leaving it ripe for myth-making. Of course, every myth needs a hero, and in America, the favorite hero is always the

rags-to-riches immigrant who succeeds by the sweat of his own brow.

But if Strauss wasn't an inventor, he was certainly an innovator, and he knew a good idea when he heard it. That's just what happened in 1872, when he was approached by a fellow tailor and dry-goods wholesaler named Jacob Davis. He *did* have a customer who complained that his pants weren't strong enough to hold heavy ore samples and always ripped at the pockets. Davis had the idea of adding rivets at the pocket corners and other points of strain, and he wanted Strauss to become his partner and put up the money to patent his design. Strauss agreed, and on May 20, 1873, the "birthday" of blue jeans, the patent was granted. Strauss and Davis went into production right away, and the pants were an instant success.

Many of the features of those early pants can still be found on some styles of Levi's jeans. The famous leather label of those two hitched horses grew out of a publicity stunt put on to prove that even workhorses couldn't tear the jeans apart. That funny little pocket in the front was added in 1890 to accommodate pocket watches. And that same year, the pants were assigned the style number 501, which is still in use today.

But it hasn't always been smooth sailing for Levi Strauss & Co. In the 1990s, the popularity of traditional jeans fell to an all-time low. Levi's had a hard time convincing young buyers that jeans were still a symbol of counterculture defiance when these were the pants their parents were wearing. The company lost a huge portion of its market, and it began to close factories and lay off workers across North America.

How do you make your product seem new and exciting when it has remained virtually the same for 130 years? That is the challenge facing all jeans manufacturers. Levi's search for the answer has led it straight to the growing market for what are called vintage and "new vintage" jeans. Vintage jeans are real, used jeans from before the 1980s, when companies began dying the pants with synthetic indigo and using a different technique to weave the fabric. These "antique" jeans are especially popular in Japan, where they can sell for thousands of

BLUE FOR BOYS

Although the method for making synthetic indigo was discovered in 1880, some jeans manufacturers continued to use the real thing for about another hundred years. Real indigo comes from a plant, a member of the pea family, and it has been used as a dye since at least the 1500s.

The legend that Levi Strauss made the first jeans by coloring canvas tent fabric with indigo dye does have some basis in reality. Indigo has long been a popular way to color clothes, primarily because blue is a good hue for covering dirt and grime. But fabrics tinted with indigo and its predecessor, woad, didn't hold their color well. The dyes tended to fade and run, so they were generally used only for workers' clothes and eventually became associated with the lower classes.

To this day, we recognize this distinction when we call people who do physical, labor-intensive jobs blue-collar workers. Office workers and professionals are called white-collar for the crisp white dress shirts they traditionally wore with their jackets and ties.

dollars. One pair of Levi's – from the 1890s, when they were supposedly lost deep in an Arizona mine – sold for $25,000!

The odder – and more lucrative – market is for "new vintage" jeans. These are replicas of "antique" jeans that sell in all of today's standard sizes for several hundred dollars apiece. Levi's has produced "new vintage" jeans that copy pairs from the 1880s to the 1930s. For the company's 130th anniversary, 501 select customers were able to purchase replicas of a patched and beat-up pair of jeans from 1917 – for $501, of course.

In producing these "new vintage" jeans, the company is trading on people's love of nostalgia. They buy these jeans because they conjure up images of a simpler time, when men were rugged and lived honestly off the fruit of the land. It's an attractive notion in an era when most of us sit behind desks or at computer screens all day, coming in contact with nature and physical labor only by accident. Perhaps this is even what helped transform jeans from blue-color work-wear into white-color officewear in the first place.

Fit to Be Tied

Wearing jeans to the office would have been unthinkable for most men just a few short decades ago, but now it's quite common. The need for both comfort and what people believe is individuality has pushed aside the dull gray and blue suits that once were everywhere and unexpectedly made room for clothes that grew out of life in a frontier town. It shows how much our ideas of acceptable dress have changed over the past fifty years. And yet some men still hold on to their neckties, arguably the most pointless item of any outfit, and one that has long been used to advertise the wearer's social standing, breeding (or lack thereof), level of education, and so on.

For a long time, historians thought men's neckwear was a seventeenth-century invention. The almost universally accepted story was that the fashion grew out of the Thirty Years' War, a long religious conflict that pitted, primarily, Sweden and France against countries of the Holy Roman Empire, especially Germany, Austria, and Bohemia (now the Czech Republic). The French king, Louis XIII, recruited Croatian soldiers to aid in his cause, and historians believed that the arrival in Paris of these soldiers, whose uniform included a lace or silk scarf tied jauntily around the neck, sparked a craze for what came to be called cravats (a corruption, or so the theory went, of the word "Croat").

But in 1974, a group of Chinese peasants who were searching for a new water source near the ancient city of Xi'an uncovered a long-forgotten cavern that led to the tomb of China's first emperor, Shi Huangdi. Although he lived in the second century B.C., Shi Huangdi advanced China in many ways, beginning construction of the Great Wall, establishing a strong central government, and standardizing the Chinese script. This warlord was bold and powerful, but he was not fearless.

He was so afraid to die, in fact, that he wanted to slaughter an entire army so the soldiers could go with him into the afterlife. Fortunately, his advisers – whose own necks might well have been on the line – convinced him that there was a better solution. They urged him to invite the best, most accomplished sculptors from across China to come to Xi'an and begin creating a terra cotta army – 7,500 life-size soldiers made entirely out of clay. It was these soldiers that the Chinese peasants stumbled across on that hot late-summer day.

A man of Shi Huangdi's standing required a fighting force – even a pretend one – that was vast and impressive. Because these terra cotta soldiers were going to travel with their emperor through eternity, they had to be exact in every detail. The sculptors painstakingly recreated the weapons and armor of the time, and they carved 7,500 different facial expressions, physical builds, and hairstyles, making each one of the soldiers unique. And yet they were also the same in one unexpected way: they all had strips of fabric tied around their necks.

What made this discovery so puzzling was that historians had thought neckwear was first worn centuries after the reign of Shi Huangdi. Even in China, there is no other known evidence of neckcloths for hundreds of years to come. So why would these soldiers have been sculpted wearing something that was clearly not an everyday part of Chinese life at that time? The answer seems to be that it was exactly because it *wasn't* a part of everyday life – the neckcloths symbolized that these soldiers (or the men who inspired them) were not like other citizens.

And so this ancient Chinese burial chamber seemed to be the origin of men's love affair with neckwear as a mark of status, a way of saying "I am better than you." Or, more specifically, "I attended a more prestigious school/ attained a higher military rank/ have more money than you." In the centuries after Shi Huangdi's reign, however, when cloth was not so easy to come by, even the wealthy couldn't afford to waste it on something that served no actual function, so this role was performed instead by increasingly elaborate necklaces and even dual-purpose hoods and cloaks. Neckcloths were pretty much forgotten.

But by the time of the Renaissance, in the 1400s and 1500s, Europe was becoming wealthier and more sophisti-
cated. Cloth was more plentiful, and men began to sport those massive collars and, in particular, ruffs that we associate with Shakespearean times. Then in the 1600s, perhaps with the appearance of those Croatian soldiers or maybe just as the result of a natural evolution in fashion, the neckcloth was rediscovered, and men had a more tasteful, modest way to announce their status.

Sometimes this desire to advertise superiority reached absurd levels. In the 1700s, for example, men began donning a kind of neckwear known as the stock. This high collar was made by wrapping fabrics like linens and silks around a frame of whalebone, pasteboard, or sometimes even wood. It was designed first for soldiers, to encourage thrusting chins and heads held high. Officers reportedly pushed their men to tighten their stocks literally to death-defying levels. Their eyes bulged, their noses bled. Fainting and even suffocation were real dangers. Not surprisingly, it was almost impossible for the men to fight with any degree of success.

As impractical as the stock was, it was soon adopted by non-military men who liked the red-faced, stiff-backed appearance it created. It was also easy to wear and durable (it could be recovered with fresh material any number of times). And those who wanted to display their individuality could choose unique fabrics and add a fancy bow or a rich-looking buckle.

But eventually the tide began to turn against the stock. Men grew tired of moving their heads with care – for fear they would accidentally cut themselves with the constricting edges of the whalebone or wood – and soon that old standby the cravat had re-emerged. Yet within a few decades, even the sensible cravat had been pushed to ridiculous new limits. Men were wrapping increasingly absurd lengths of fabric around their necks and up as high as their ears, sometimes even covering their mouths. There were so many complicated ways to tie all this material that publishers soon realized there was money to be made in instructional books for the baffled and bewildered. One of these, *The Art of Tying the Cravat*, became a bestseller throughout Europe.

Apart from being a guide to mastering the thirty-two different knot styles that existed at the time, *The Art of Tying the Cravat* was also a history of the neckwear craze. While acknowl-

edging that the mania sometimes got out of hand, the author recounted the story of one man whose cravat was so immense and draped the neck in so much protective fabric that it was able to stop a bullet that would surely have ended his life had he been more modestly dressed. And he wasn't the only one to maintain there was a protective function to the humble neck-cloth. As late as the 1870s, doctors were claiming that men who rejected their cravats in favor of low collars and bow ties risked death from chilly winter blasts.

Today's modern necktie, called the four-in-hand, originated in the 1860s, when men began to need neckwear that suited their more active lives. One day some enterprising fellow, perhaps tired of having his neckcloth come loose at a crucial juncture in his cricket match, simply untied his cravat and reknotted it like the reins of a four-in-hand carriage (it would have looked something like a Boy Scout scarf). That simple modification was the origin of the modern tie; in fact, all the neckties men can buy today are based on styles that have been around since the 1870s.

The four-in-hand was less fussy and expensive than the cravat, and therefore quickly embraced by the rising Victorian middle class. But of course it wouldn't do to have everyone looking the same, so the upper crust created the idea of school ties, club ties, regimental ties, and the list goes on. With one glance, anyone who knew what to look for could tell what kind of school your parents had been able to afford, which branch of the military you served and what rank you attained, or whether you had rowed for Oxford or Cambridge. Some London merchants even refused to sell certain regimental ties without proof that their customers had the right to wear them, a practice that continues to this day.

Even though many modern men claim they wear ties to express their individuality – you can buy them patterned with golf balls or cartoon characters or the logo of your favorite hockey team – the truth is that the tie is still a mark of class distinction and social status, just as it was in Shi Huangdi's time. For men who have hard, physical jobs or just work a lot with their hands, it simply isn't practical to wear one; any tie, no matter how silly its pattern, marks you as a white-collar worker who is willing to put up with a little discomfort to prove it.

Hanky-Panky

In the Thirteen Colonies, where there was slightly less interest in class divisions and considerably more need for comfortable, affordable fashions, the bandanna was the neckwear of choice. Imported from India via England and made of silk, the first bandannas in the New World were actually just handkerchiefs being put to a new use.

Surprisingly, the handkerchief is one of our more ancient items of clothing. For about fifteen centuries, starting in roughly 1000 B.C., hankies were in almost continuous use. But then came the period in Europe known as the Dark Ages (about 450 to 900 A.D.). During those terrible times, people lost a lot of the knowledge and customs that had been acquired in previous centuries. Many ancient skills were forgotten, and few Europeans got any formal schooling. Manners, good taste, and personal hygiene all fell by the wayside.

When it came to clothing, one of the first casualties was the handkerchief. Most Dark Agers reverted to using sleeves, the backs of hands, and whatever else was close by to wipe noses, mop sweaty brows, and dab tearing eyes (and we probably don't want to know what else!). Fortunately, the rediscovery of the handkerchief didn't take long. By 1100 or so, it was back in general circulation, and it remained an essential accessory for both men and women until the 1920s, when the first boxes of Kleenex rolled off the production line.

But those disposable tissues are a poor substitute for the multi-purpose hanky, which, at various points in history, has been used not only to keep people looking presentable but also to signal the start of a race, to symbolize an engagement between a man and a

THE BETTER TO SEE YOU WITH

For centuries, people whose eyesight began to decline had no hope for improvement. One ancient writer was rumored to have kept up his reading by using a glass globe of water to magnify the words, but most people just squinted their way through life. That all mercifully changed in the late 1200s, when eyeglasses were invented.

Of course, glasses weren't all that practical until someone came up with an effective way to hold them on the face. Many methods were tried, including ribbons that could be tied at the back of the head and weighted strings that would hang down over the ears, before a workable eyeglass frame was finally devised.

By the 1400s, glasses were a popular fashion accessory. They were also a symbol of status, because they were costly to buy and would usually be worn only by those who could read. But soon they became associated with age and failing faculties, and people grew more self-conscious about wearing them. Some glasses-wearers still feel that way today, but now many bespectacled trend-setters own multiple pairs that they change almost as often as they change their clothes.

woman, and to express an audience's delight at the theater.

Like so many other items of clothing, the handkerchief was also useful for distinguishing the haves from the have-nots. The ancient Persians decreed that only nobles and other high-born citizens could carry them, for example, and in Rome, the hankies of the well-to-do were often elaborately decorated and made of finer fabrics, the better to differentiate them from the vulgar rags of those lower down the social ladder.

During the American Civil War, hankies took on a whole new meaning. With the death rate of some battles nearing 25 percent, a soldier often went off to fight having printed his name and address on a handkerchief and pinned it to his uniform. These were essentially the first dog tags, and they could be used to identify the dead when the battle was over. They might also have done double duty as white flags of surrender when it became clear that all was lost.

Lovesick Victorians discovered a less grim use for hankies in the 1890s. In those staid and conservative times, it was very difficult for men and women who weren't married to communicate openly with each other. Public displays of affection were out of the question, and even the simple act of conversation between the sexes was frowned upon. Such restrictions made it a challenge for young men to woo and win young ladies, until a few clever souls invented a whole set of nonverbal messages that could be sent via the hanky across a crowded room. A gentleman who drew his handkerchief across his lips was telling a lady he would like to make her acquaintance. She might signal back by resting her own hanky on her right cheek for yes or her left cheek for

no. If she wanted to be more firm in her refusal, she could draw her hanky through her hand – the sign for "I hate you" – or twist it in her right hand – for "I love someone else." In all, there were about two dozen messages that could be sent this way.

Today, the handkerchief has mostly passed quietly into disuse, and with it has gone this wonderful unspoken language and so much of the formality in men's dress. We cannot count on a man's outfit revealing to us his entire personal history as it once would have done. Now the well-off are as likely as anyone else to wear torn, patched jeans and T-shirts advertising soft drinks or clothing stores. As one author described it, we have had to learn to read through the rips to distinguish those with power from those without. Clothes, perhaps, no longer make the man.

Topping it All Off

Samson was a man whose strength was legendary. The Bible tells us that he could fight off whole armies single-handedly, and that he once killed a thousand of his enemies, the Philistines, with the jawbone of an ass. Even today, people associate him with superhuman power.

Because of a vow sworn by his parents before his birth, Samson was never to drink wine or eat the grapes it was made from, touch a dead body, or most famously, cut a hair on his head. He didn't take those vows too seriously, however, and in time he broke all but the last one. This he kept because he knew his hair was the source of his great strength.

Unfortunately, Samson wasn't much better at choosing women than he was at keeping promises. When he fell in love with Delilah, a Philistine beauty, she tricked him into revealing the secret of his strength and then cut off all his hair while he slept. When he woke up, he was set upon by Philistine soldiers, who easily captured the newly shorn Samson, blinded him, and put him to work as a slave. He was often placed on display, to be mocked and taunted by the Philistine people. It was a terrible life of daily humiliation and torture that offered Samson no hope of escape until his hair eventually grew back. At last reinvested with the might of several men, he was able to topple the walls of a great temple full of Philistines. His strength had returned, but at a terrible price. Three thousand people – including Samson himself – were killed.

Hair Today, Gone Tomorrow

Samson's story reminds us of the great power we attach to our hair. In his case, the power was physical. For the rest of us, it might be power of a subtler kind: an ability to attract mates, a sign that we are young and healthy, evidence of our wealth and position in society. We have, for centuries, spent fortunes in both money and time on

our hair – cutting it, styling it, shaving it off and letting it grow, curling it and coloring it, even hiding it away beneath hats, scarves, and wigs.

Our obsession with our hair goes back to prehistoric times. Primitive men liked to smear their locks with mud or clay and tie on small trophies for added effect. For many ancient people, whose style of dress tended to be simple and unadorned, hair provided an important opportunity to display status and individuality. Hairpins, wigs,

THE LONG AND THE SHORT OF IT

The length of a man's hair was often regulated by law or custom. And more often than not, nobles were on one side of the issue and the clergy on the other.

Throughout European history, battles were waged between aristocrats who liked to wear their hair long and religious leaders who wanted it kept short. England's Henry I let his hair grow in long ringlets down his back, a look that so angered the archbishop of Canterbury that he threatened to excommunicate any Church members who followed this lead. Fortunately for Henry, he outlived the archbishop by a quarter-century – and conveniently forgot to appoint the man's successor for many years.

France's Louis VII, more loyal to the Church than Henry, cropped his locks exactly as the Vatican desired. Sadly, it wasn't what his free-spirited wife, Eleanor of Guyenne, desired. She detested his monk-like appearance and the personality that went with it, and quickly left him, taking with her the rich provinces of west-central France that had been her dowry. Soon after, she married the man who would become England's Henry II, handing her land over to him. This launched a period of bloody conflict between England and France that would last for centuries.

extensions, bleaches, waxes, and oils were all used to accentuate the positive and mask the negative. The Egyptians even experimented with treatments for that fear of men both ancient and modern: baldness. One "cure" advised sufferers to coat their heads with chopped lettuce leaves to stimulate growth. Bald men were also encouraged to rub their pates with the fats of lions, hippopotamuses, crocodiles, cats, serpents, and goats. There was no advice on how they were to acquire these fats – or how long they had to wear what must surely have been a pretty unpleasant concoction.

The Egyptians were a vain lot all around. If baldness wasn't an issue, they found other hair-related worries to occupy their minds. We know, for example, that they were among the first to use dye to cover tell-tale gray. As early as 3400 B.C., they were apparently using henna, a dye extracted from a small shrub, to give their hair a reddish hue. Indigo, another dye derived from plant material, was applied to produce that blue-black color we often associate with these ancient people.

But the Egyptians were not the only ones to understand the value of an attractive head of hair. The Babylonians spared no expense in their quest to look good, powdering their locks with real gold dust. Ancient Saxons dyed their hair blue using woad, yet another dye made from a plant; Saxon women also used an ointment of burnt bear claws and swallow droppings to give their hair a glossy sheen. The Romans were so fond of their hair that it took on an almost spiritual significance. Some washed their locks only once a year, fearful that too much cleansing would scrub away the gods who protected them. And the first haircut was of such ritual importance to Roman boys that the auspicious event was recorded at city hall.

The idea that hair has some kind of magical or spiritual significance has persisted in different cultures – including ours – through the centuries. Sikhs, for instance, view hair as sacred. Throughout their lives, devout followers of Sikhism are prohibited from removing even a single hair from their bodies. They would no more cut their hair than they would remove an arm or a leg. For the ancient Greeks, hair was such a strong symbol that people would shave their heads when in mourning or decorate their doors with a lock from the deceased. We practice a less morbid version of this act of remembrance when we carry about a piece of a loved one's hair in a locket or press a baby's hair in a memory book.

To shave a person's head against his will, as happened to Samson, also has great significance. Almost always, it's an act meant to humiliate. Since ancient times, victorious armies have shaved their conquered enemies bald, a ritual that had the dual effect of degrading them and announcing their defeat to the world. Even though we have today lost many of the rites associated with hair, this is one that survives. We still shave the heads of prisoners and soldiers as the first step in a campaign to break them down and rebuild them as better models. And in France after the Second World War, women who had collaborated with the Nazis were shaved bald and paraded through the streets, their humiliation and betrayal on display for all to see.

Flipping Your Wig

Of course, if you have been shaved or otherwise lost your mane, you always have the option of hiding your hairless state with a hat, a scarf, or the ever-popular wig. Wigs, especially, have a long history in fashion. The ancient Egyptians, both men and women, were especially fond of them and took them along even into the afterworld. For them, wigs served a practical purpose: they often shaved all the hair off their heads (and even their entire bodies), and so needed something to cover themselves with. This was not vanity but a logical solution to the very real problem of an unforgiving African sun. Wigs were removable and allowed for better air circulation, so they were both cooler to wear than real hair and a good alternative to the sweaty, greasy locks that were common in the days before shampoo and daily showers.

Among the women of ancient Rome, blonde hair was the thing to have. This look became popular around 1 A.D., when Roman gladiators returned from northern Europe with fair-haired slaves they had taken as the spoils of war. Seeing the amorous excitement these flaxen-haired women produced in their husbands, Roman wives began to look for ways to go blonde themselves. Some tried dyes made from yellow flowers, while those who could afford it simply dusted their locks with powdered gold. But for many, the easiest solution was also the most obvious: they merely cut off the locks of the captured slaves and had that hair made into thick, full wigs for themselves.

Wigs didn't really catch on in most of Europe until the 1600s, and then they were worn almost exclusively by men. (Most women didn't begin wearing them until the next century.) They first became popular in France, when Louis XIII disguised his baldness with a wig of dark, rich curls that fell gracefully past his shoulders and down his back. The craze soon spread to other parts of Europe, and wig-wearing remained fashionable there (and eventually in America) for the next 150 years.

Louis's curls were meant to be taken for his own, but soon the trend was to wear white powdered wigs, sometimes called periwigs. The white color had several advantages: it masked the join where false hair met real; it disguised wigs that were of inferior quality; and it mimicked lighter-colored hair, which was the fashion at the time. The powder was made of ground starch or even plaster of Paris, and sometimes it would be scented with lavender or orange. As the trend grew, more

vibrant colors were also used, including blues, violets, yellows, and pinks.

The seventeenth-century craze for wigs knew no limits. Even when rumors began to circulate that unscrupulous wigmakers were creating their wares from the infected hair of dead plague victims, people went right on wearing them. There were good reasons why. As in ancient Egypt, wigs were a much better option than greasy, seldom-washed hair, and they also helped curb the spread of head lice. The best wigs were reserved for the aristocracy, of course, but even men in the lower classes wore them if they wanted to be considered stylish. Those who couldn't afford wigs made from real human hair had to accept poor substitutes made from horsehair, goat hair, and even the hair of yaks. One writer has referred to wig-wearing as "an ingenious conspiracy of the elderly, the moneyed, and the ungifted," because it meant that even those with full, beautiful hair (usually the young) had to cover it if they wanted to keep up with the times.

THE WIGMAKER'S CRAFT

While the wigs of the Egyptians were often highly ornamented and colored an artificial-looking bluish black, the Romans, like modern-day wig aficionados, wanted people to believe their wigs were really their own hair. They started the trend of creating hairpieces that don't look like hairpieces at all.

Wig-making is a true art, and realistic-looking wigs are justifiably expensive because they take many hours to make and require constant upkeep when done. When using human hair, the wigmaker must first clean it and sort it. (For a wig to look good, every single strand in it must go in the same direction.) Then he begins the tedious job of sewing the hair to a piece of netting, a process that takes about forty hours and involves making thirty to forty thousand tiny knots. Once all that is done, the wig still needs to be cut and styled.

We have been making wigs this way since the 1600s. Even though we now have high-quality artificial hair, wigs made from human hair are still the most desirable. Today most of what's used is bleached hair from the Asian market, where it sells for about a thousand dollars a pound (two thousand dollars a kilogram).

By the time the eighteenth century drew to a close, the fashion for wigs had begun to die out. In France, where the hairpieces were so closely associated with the aristocracy, the end came with the French Revolution (1789–99). No one wanted to be caught in a wig in that turbulent society, where to wear one could spell a trip to the guillotine. In America, too, wigs became linked in people's minds to the wealthy and privileged (and British), even though they were commonly worn in colonial times by widely admired men like George Washington and John Adams. After the American Revolution, colonists wanted to rid their society of all things "undemocratic" (and British), so wigs just had to go. In England, however, the demise of the wig was caused by a much less dramatic event than a revolution; there, an ill-considered tax on hair powder was the final nail in the proverbial coffin.

Most of us don't wear wigs any more. For the most part, we prefer to work with what we've been given, cutting, straightening, curling, dyeing, and styling our own tresses. We do sometimes opt for hair extensions; these are pieces of human hair that are color-matched and then glued and woven in place to give our own hair a fuller or longer appearance. And for men who are balding and wish to try to hide the fact, there's always the trusty toupée; like hair extensions, the best toupées should look just like a person's natural hair.

But most wigs today are worn primarily by actors and other performers, or by people who have lost their hair because of illness. Wigs have even come under attack in the British court system, where they have long been part of the costume of judges and lawyers. In the late 1980s, some barristers with no sense of tradition began promoting the idea that these wigs should be abolished. They banded together in a group called Lawyers Against Wigs and launched a vigorous – but ultimately unsuccessful – protest against the hairpieces on the grounds that they made them look ridiculous.

To Shave or Not to Shave

All this talk of hair leads us quite naturally to the question of shaving, which we tend to think of as a relatively modern custom. In our minds, prehistoric men ran around with woolly beards and unkempt locks, hardly distinguishable from the beasts they hunted. There is some evidence, however, in the form of cave paintings, that as early as 100,000 B.C. men used clam shells to pluck out facial hair. We know for certain that razors made of sharpened stones were in use by 30,000 B.C.

What makes men choose a hairy state over a hairless one, or vice versa? It can be any one of a number of things: religion, social standing, the preferences of the fairer sex, a need to cover a blemish or other facial imperfection, a desire to conform or (at other times) not to conform. As long as there have been civilizations, men have been

alternately shaving and growing facial hair to meet one or more of these requirements.

The ancients enjoyed a nice beard, which they took as a sign of wisdom and knowledge. Egyptian kings wore the longest ones in their society, and high-ranking men *and* women would don fake beards of gold or silver for special festivals and celebrations. The Greeks also favored beards – at least until the fourth century B.C. and the reign of Alexander the Great. He ordered his soldiers to be clean-shaven because he didn't want the enemy to have anything to grab hold of during close, hand-to-hand fighting. In both these societies, the poor slaves got the short end of the stick, as usual. When the fashion was to wear a beard, they were forced to shave (sometimes their heads as well as their beards), and when the fashion was to be clean-shaven, they had to sprout whiskers on demand. In effect, they were made to advertise their low social status on their faces.

The Romans were originally beard-ed too, and like the Egyptians, they would wear false whiskers for special occasions. But in the third century B.C., barbers began to set up shop on the streets of Rome, and soon shaving was the thing to do. The barbershops even did double duty as social clubs and gossip mills. Very quickly, the act of shaving took on a ritualistic significance. Roman boys would let their beards grow unchecked until they reached adulthood, when they would shave and present their shorn whiskers as an offering to the gods. The clean-shaven look remained popular until the reign of Hadrian (117–38 A.D.), who report-edly wore a beard to cover facial scars and warts. That was enough to bring whiskers back in fashion once again.

For some, facial hair, or its lack, has had religious significance. The prophet Muhammad, the founder of Islam, urged his followers to let their beards grow. Among Muslims, shaving was considered sinful, perhaps because a clean-shaven face was thought to be too feminine. Christian clergymen in Rome also originally wore beards, but their Greek equivalents did not. When the Church split into its Eastern Orthodox and Western halves in the eleventh century, the roles were reversed. To this day, Greek Orthodox priests still favor long beards, while Roman Catholics are more likely to be clean-shaven. And of course, when

Protestantism rose up in the 1500s as an alternative to Catholicism, its leaders embraced the beard as a sign of their nonconformity. And the circle continues.

Sometimes the obsession with facial hair seemed to get a little out of control. In parts of sixteenth-century Europe, men wore their beards so long that they would have to wrap the ends around their waists like a belt to be able to walk. In Russia, Peter the Great's prohibition against whiskers resulted in a beard tax. If you wanted to keep your chin-warmer, you'd have to pay the small toll and carry around a copper disk that was, in effect, a beard license. In 1535, England's Henry VIII also imposed a beard tax – while maddeningly continuing to sport one himself.

Soon, men were doing a lot more to their beards than simply letting them grow or shaving them off. Facial hair began to be powdered, colored, perfumed, starched – even curled with curling irons and shaped into new styles. Some men would sleep with their beards in bags or sandwiched in wooden presses to try to protect all the hard work they'd put in to styling them. Not wanting to be left out, the clean-shaven soon had their own arsenal

of hair-related products, from rust-resistant razors to shaving creams. The ever-fashionable French may have given the most to the art of shaving, inventing both the shaving brush (in 1748) and the safety razor (in 1770).

In the nineteenth century, facial hair seemed to regain its old status as a mark of wisdom and intellect. No political figure or business leader could hope to succeed without a beard, a mustache, or long bushy sideburns. But by the 1900s, the pendulum had swung again. There was too much money to

SHAVE AND A HAIRCUT

It's well known that barbers used to perform some types of surgery. Even today the familiar red-and-white-striped barber pole (white for clean bandages, red for bloody) reminds us of this fact. It's possible that this practice began in the twelfth century, when the clergy decided that drawing blood was a desecration of the human body. From that point on, barbers had to take over all the bloodletting (whereby sick people would have some blood drained in an attempt to draw out infection or disease).

Leeches were the tool of choice for bloodletting, perhaps because they were easier to use and less painful than the scalpel-like lancet, which was also common. (Even the leeches are memorialized in the barber pole: the brass ball on top was once a bowl that held the parasites when they were not being used.) But few self-respecting barbers limited themselves to bloodletting. From the 1100s until the late 1700s, customers could engage in an early form of one-stop shopping, getting their teeth pulled, their boils lanced, or their wounds dressed along with a trim and a shave. It wasn't until trained surgeons banded together in protest that this practice was halted. That and a few misplaced cuts in the chair effectively put the barber-surgeons out of business.

be made from disposable razors to allow the bearded look to persist; even women, who alas had no beards to shave, were led to believe that removing their underarm and leg hair was an absolute necessity. In fact, except for a defiant resurgence of beards in the 1960s, the clean-shaven look has predominated to this day. Modern women prefer clean-shaven men by a massive margin, and we have even become convinced, all logic aside, that the hairless look is the more manly one.

Whether we wear it short or long, on our faces or our heads, to fit in or to stand out, our hair always makes a statement. It is the one physical feature that we can change at will, without submitting to the surgeon's knife. Straight hair that's suddenly curled or a beard that's unexpectedly shaved off can have a huge, instant impact on our appearance. And if we're not happy with our new look . . . well, we need only wait a few weeks for the perm to grow out or the new beard to grow in. Fortunately for us, hair is remarkably forgiving of all our sudden impulses.

Accessories After the Fact

Prometheus was the world's first troublemaker. When Zeus, ruler of all the gods in Greek mythology, decided he wanted to punish mortal men by denying them fire, Prometheus climbed to the heavens, lit a torch from the sun, and came back to earth bearing the element as a gift. Having fire was important because it was one of the first things that distinguished humans from animals; fire also offered a protection more valuable than speed or courage or strength, qualities that – according to myth – had all been passed out to the animals before human beings were ever created.

Zeus was understandably furious that he had been undermined, but Prometheus wasn't finished yet. He plotted to cheat the gods again by giving mortals the best parts of any animal sacrificed. He cut up an ox, wrapping all the good meat in the unappetizing hide and covering all the bones and gristle in shimmering, delicious-looking fat. Then he asked Zeus to choose between the two. A little slow on the uptake, Zeus chose what turned out to be the pile of worthless bones. This time, his anger could not be suppressed. He ordered Prometheus chained to a rock on a remote, lonely mountaintop for three thousand years. Every day, an eagle would come to devour his liver, and every night, the liver would grow back to its usual size.

Of course, three thousand years is a very long time to hold a grudge, and eventually Zeus decided that Prometheus had learned his lesson and could be set free. But Zeus wanted to remind him of the punishment that was in store if he crossed the gods again. So he decreed that Prometheus must wear around his finger a link of the chain that had once bound him to the mountaintop. This "ring" – the very first fashion accessory – would be a constant reminder of the dangers of playing with fire.

Rings on Your Fingers, Bells on Your Toes

Prometheus never really existed, of course, but one thing about his story is most certainly true: people have been wearing jewelry since ancient times. Even prehistoric men and women donned crude necklaces and bracelets made of leather and decorated with animal bones, shells, and feathers. When the Bronze Age began, about 3500 B.C., women started to make metal disks and rings and use them to stretch out their necks, mouths, and earlobes. Instead of trying to add to their natural beauty, these women wanted to make themselves as unappealing as possible so they would be passed over by potential captors. This custom is still practiced among the Mursi of southern Ethiopia. As children, the female members of this tribe have their lower lips split and their bottom front teeth removed to make room for a small clay disk. This first disk is replaced with progressively larger versions as the women, more commonly known as disk-lip women, age and their lips become more and more slack. Eventually, the disks can be almost equal in size to the woman's face.

Just as in prehistoric times, the point of the disk lip was originally to make the women seem unappealing. The practice was introduced long ago by Mursi men who hoped to protect their women from slave traders. Today the tables have been turned and the disk lips are a symbol of beauty and affluence. Now the size of the disk reportedly represents the number of cattle the girl's father will give as her dowry when she marries. Some girls, to make themselves even more desirable, also pierce their earlobes, stretching them to their chins with disks that match!

Like the disk-lip women, many of us wear jewelry in the hope that it will attract the attention of potential mates. But we also use it as a sign of wealth and status, and sometimes we wear it for religious reasons. Traditionally, jewelry has also had superstitious associations. People have worn bracelets, necklaces, and earrings to ward off evil spirits or summon good fortune.

The Egyptians – those connoisseurs of all things fashionable – took the lead, as they so often did, in the making and wearing of jewelry. They used both gold and silver extensively, and they were probably the first to incorporate semi-precious stones like lapis lazuli, turquoise, and garnet. For wealthy royal women, the must-have fashion accessory was the broad collar. Hundreds of small, colorful stone beads would be strung together in a semi-circular collar that covered the chest, neck, and shoulders. Many of these collars were so intricate and so heavy that they required a counterpoise, a weight that hung down the wearer's back to help her keep her balance. Earrings were also a popular choice, for everyone from mature women to young boys. Some later tomb paintings even show the family cat sporting a fine pair of delicate gold hoops.

The Egyptians were so attached to their baubles and trinkets that they had to invent the first costume (in other words, fake) jewelry. Like the plastic jewelry we wear today, these fake pieces, made of ground quartz and mineral glaze, could be molded into a variety of shapes and dyed different colors to mimic more expensive stones. This very democratic innovation meant that even the poorest members of Egyptian society could strut about in what looked like real jewels.

Roman society wasn't nearly so charitable. Lacking the riches of the

IN THE EYE OF THE BEHOLDER

In the quest for beauty, we often go to extreme lengths. But perhaps nothing seems quite as extreme as the beauty practices of the Padaung women of Burma, who engage in a custom called neck-stretching.

When a Padaung girl is just five or six, she will be fitted with the first of several bronze neck rings. Once every two years or so, more rings will be added, and by the time the girl is ready to marry, her neck will be about ten inches (25 centimeters) longer than normal. The more numerous the rings, the greater the status of the girl's family within the tribe.

In fact, the girl's neck isn't actually being stretched. Instead, the weight of the rings causes her shoulders to collapse, giving the appearance of a longer neck. The Padaung men, like their Mursi counterparts, reportedly introduced neck-stretching as a way of making their women undesirable to slave traders. But the practice also serves as a means of control. Some husbands forcibly remove the rings when they suspect their wives of being unfaithful. With weakened necks no longer supported by the rings, these women risk suffocation and, in some extreme cases, will have to spend the rest of their lives lying down if they want to keep breathing.

Egyptians in the early days of their civilization, the Romans decided that only the wealthy could wear gold jewelry; all those lower down the social ladder had to make do with silver or, if they were really poor, iron. Later, when Rome had conquered many other nations and grown into a financial powerhouse, gold was restricted because there was too much of it. It simply wouldn't do for the poor or – worse yet – slaves to go about flashing their gold rings and looking as though they could be important. Even unmarried women were told they could no longer wear jewelry – a ban that sent many running to the altar.

Roman men were probably the first to give their girlfriends rings to symbolize an engagement. This practice was picked up by the Egyptians, Greeks, and eventually early Christians. In time, it evolved into our modern custom of exchanging wedding bands. The ring, a perfect circle, was the obvious choice as a symbol for a life partnership; circles have no beginnings and no ends, so they represent eternity. A Roman wife would wear her ring on the fourth finger of her left hand, just as we do today. The belief was that the veins of this finger led directly to the

heart. Of course, since most people are right-handed, there's also an assumption that the left hand is the weaker, less able one. (In fact, our modern English word "sinister" comes from the Latin for "left.") Only women were required to advertise their marriages on their left ring fingers, and we have to wonder if, in those ancient, male-dominated societies, the equating of women with weakness and even bad fortune was entirely an accident.

Rings have also been used to symbolize authority. Signet rings, for exam-ple, have since at least the Middle Ages been an acceptable substitute for a person's signature. Engraved with the wearer's family crest or some symbol of his profession, the ring could be pressed into wax to seal a contract or finalize a business deal. To steal a per-son's signet ring was a serious crime, sort of an early form of what we today call identity theft.

Some rings have been used to iden-tify people who have achieved a special status or rank. Each new pope, for example, is given a ring bearing an

47

image of St. Peter in a fishing boat. When the pope dies – that is, the circle of his life comes to an end – the ring is destroyed and a new one crafted for his successor. Those fortunate enough to meet the pope are expected to kiss this ring as a sign of submission and respect. This custom was picked up by members of the Mafia, who require those lower down in the organization to kiss their rings for the same reasons.

Today we use rings to mark special achievements or as evidence of our membership in certain groups. Athletes vie for Super Bowl or World Series rings, and high-school seniors covet graduation rings. In Canada, all engineering graduates are given iron rings in memory of the Quebec Bridge disaster of 1907. That year, a steel bridge collapsed under its own weight because of design flaws, killing dozens of workers. The rings, which many people believe were originally made from the wreckage of the collapsed bridge, remind all engineers that they have a responsibility to ensure that the disaster is never repeated. For a little added romance, the ring itself is roughly crafted. Over the years, its edges begin to wear smooth, just like the rough edges of a young engineer's mind,

which are softened with the maturity and wisdom that come with age.

The Gloves Are Off

Although rings have been popular since ancient times, there was a long period when – thanks to another fashion accessory – they were seldom seen.

Hand coverings of some kind were probably first worn in prehistoric times by cave dwellers. They were a purely practical, functional item of clothing that may have evolved into a version of our modern glove with fingers as early as the time of ancient Egypt. Gloves were at their most popular from the 1200s to the 1800s, but people continued to wear them routinely right up to the 1960s. Today gloves are used primarily by athletes like cyclists and sailors, health professionals like doctors and nurses, and people who do physical labor and want to protect their hands. Of course, they can also be a tool of the trade for criminals who don't want to leave tell-tale fingerprints behind. Those of us who are lucky enough to live in a four-season climate also know the value of a good pair of gloves when the temperature drops below freezing.

At one point, during the Middle Ages, most people in Europe wore mittens, the idea of gloves with fingers having been lost somewhere in time. But in 1175, England's Henry II reintroduced gloves as we know them today. From then on, the less graceful mitten was left to the wardrobes of children and members of the lower classes; for those with more refined taste, fingers were the only way to go.

Over the decades, the length of glove fingers grew to the point that they soon bore no relation to the actual size of the wearer's hand. Long fingers were thought to be more elegant and genteel, and so gloves were rou-

tinely made quite a bit longer than necessary. Often, they were also embroidered with complex designs, covered with small gems or beads, or doused with perfumes and oils. If the person wearing the gloves had a particularly spectacular ring to flaunt, he or she might sport a pair with a hole cut out for the gem to peek through.

Gloves have always been highly symbolic. Before we had property deeds, people would exchange gloves to signify the transfer of land. In some wedding ceremonies, the groom would give one glove to the father of the bride, a sign of his intention to care for his wife single-handedly. And perhaps most famously, men would throw down a gauntlet, a heavy glove covered with plates of steel or iron, when they

49

had been insulted and wanted to challenge the offender to a duel.

Glove-wearers could send subtle messages simply by leaving their gloves on or taking them off. As a sign of respect, most men would remove their gloves when shaking hands. But for a woman – perceived to be more modest and proper – touching bare skin to bare skin was unthinkable. The same was true of servants, who wouldn't dare to "contaminate" their employers by brushing them with an ungloved hand.

Although we don't wear gloves as often any more, some of their symbolism has survived in our everyday speech. Two politicians who have finished being polite to each other will "drop their gloves" and lower the level of debate. A person who operates "with the gloves off" shows no compassion for others. And an item of clothing that seems made just for us is said to "fit like a glove," a reference to the way they, like shoes, begin to conform to the shape of a person's body over time.

Made in the Shade

On rare occasions, gloves have been used for decidedly sinister purposes.

Some people believe that Jeanne D'Albret, the mother of France's King Henri IV, was murdered when she pulled on a pair of perfumed gloves that had been coated with poison. And this is not the only case of a seemingly harmless fashion accessory being used as a lethal weapon. At a London bus stop one late-summer day in 1978, a Bulgarian journalist and outspoken critic of his country's Communist dictator was jabbed in the leg with the tip of an umbrella and injected with a deadly poison called ricin; he was the victim of an assassination by the Bulgarian secret police.

Like gloves, the umbrella is a fashion accessory that has been reduced from a symbol of elegance and taste to a mere practical defense against the elements. It was introduced as long as three thousand years ago by those ever-inventive Egyptians. In those days, it was used as a parasol to help people escape the blazing North African heat. (The word *parasol* comes from Latin and means "to protect from the sun.") Like so many other items of clothing, parasols could be carried only by people who had achieved a certain status in Egyptian society. When their popularity spread to other hot countries, and they began to be made with beads and fringes and in a variety of colors, additional restrictions were needed. Yellow parasols, for instance, might be permitted only to those who had earned the right to carry them by climbing high enough on the social ladder.

In northern Europe, where the problem was rain, not sun, the umbrella, or *parapluie* (French for "to protect from the rain"), was unaccountably slow to catch on. In the 1660s, it was finally introduced to England by Catherine of Braganza, the bride of Charles II. If ever a country needed umbrellas, it was England, and although Catherine's was actually a parasol from her native Portugal, Englishwomen soon saw its value for their rainy nation.

It still wouldn't do for a man to carry one, however. When one brave soul named Jonas Hanway first ventured out into the streets of London with his umbrella in the 1750s, he became an object of ridicule, reportedly followed everywhere he went by jeering street urchins. The poor man received especially bad treatment at the hands of coachmen, who suspected that Hanway's bizarre contraption represented a major threat to their livelihood. But eventually he was joined by other like-minded men, and in the

end – having endured the taunts and insults for some thirty years – Hanway had established a British institution that lives on to this day.

The parasol, meanwhile, died out when a mania for suntanning emerged in the early 1920s. Where once women went to great lengths to avoid exposing their lily white skin to the sun, they suddenly began to covet the brown hues that were the new hallmark of the rich and famous. That fad didn't diminish until the 1990s, when we first learned of the dangers of ultraviolet radiation. Perhaps now that tanned skin is no longer in vogue, the parasol will make a comeback.

Hats Off!

Despite Jonas Hanway's best efforts, some men just never took to the umbrella, perhaps because they felt there was something a little too feminine about it. A "real man" didn't mind getting wet; if necessary, he would take refuge beneath the brim of a hat, but never under an umbrella. Fortunately, the man of fashion has always had a lot of choice when it comes to hats. This is yet another acces-

sory that has been with us since ancient times, and the hat's long life has allowed a vast range of styles to develop.

One of the earliest hat styles was the Phrygian cap. This simple toque-like hat was originally given to Greek and Roman slaves when they gained their freedom, and except in countries where the turban and fez were popular, it's the only hat most men wore for hundreds of years. The Phrygian cap is also a perfect example of the strong symbolic associations hats can have. It became so identified with liberty and independence that it was adopted by French revolutionaries many centuries after it was first introduced.

What eventually replaced the Phrygian cap was the hood. By the 1100s, men had realized that the simple cap was inadequate for the job of distinguishing rich from poor. The hood, however, was more versatile. Professionals like doctors and lawyers would wear hoods of special shapes to represent their occupations. This was a practice so often copied by impostors, however, that it reportedly gave rise to the word "falsehood," which we still use today to mean a lie or untruth. "Hoodwink" is another still-common term we inherited from these times.

Thieves would hoodwink their victims, or pull down their hoods to cover their eyes, so they could rob them without being seen. Today the word means to trick or deceive someone.

Over the decades, hoods became more and more elaborate, offering added proof that men can rival women when it comes to foolish fashion trends. By the 1300s, the hood had evolved into the liripipe, which did for head coverings what a shoe called the poulaine was doing for footwear at about the same time. The liripipe was really an elongated hood; the cowl, or the back of the hood, grew ridiculously long, eventually draping as low as the wearer's ankles. Some men took to wrapping the ends of the liripipe around their head like a turban to make it easier to sit and move around. Others padded their liripipes with horsehair or hay and waggled them at passing women in a suggestive manner, whether to their delight or annoyance, we can only guess.

But women were not about to be outdone. In the fifteenth century, they latched on to their own faddish head covering, the hennin. This truly bizarre creation was something like a towering fez or a cone. Trimmed with lace and

draped with veils, the hennin could add three or more feet (more than 90 centimeters) to a woman's height. Builders reportedly had to raise doorways so the high-hatted women could get through. And of course, no one who wore such an outlandish and impractical hat could hope to be able to work or get about without the help of servants.

From hennins to fezzes to wimples to turbans, hats have inspired in us a variety of emotions, from religious piety and nationalistic fervor to rage and even hysteria. When James Hetherington, a hatter by trade, first appeared on the streets of eighteenth-century London in a black, silk-like top hat, he apparently caused a riot. Onlookers were so scandalized by this

LIFTING THE VEIL

The most symbolic of all head coverings is the veil. First worn in ancient times, it still represents modesty, humility, and submission. It is most often seen in societies where, for religious reasons, women's hair is viewed as provocative and therefore must be kept hidden. In more restrictive cultures, the whole face is covered, and there are serious, brutal consequences for women who, through carelessness or defiance, fail to keep themselves concealed.

In Western societies, veils have generally been worn less for modesty and more to attract attention. In the Middle Ages and during the Renaissance, women all over Europe draped their headwear with brightly colored veils of linen or silk, the more elaborate the better. This was also the period when Western women began to wear bridal veils. That custom dates back to ancient Rome, where it was feared that evil spirits, envious of the happy couple, might try to ruin the wedding ceremony. For the bride's own protection, she was veiled to disguise her identity. Over time, the bridal veil also came to represent innocence and purity. In some non-Western societies, where arranged marriages are more common, the first time the groom ever sees his bride is when he lifts her veil after the ceremony is over.

racy new head covering that many screamed and some even fainted. Those who were slightly more able to keep their wits chased Hetherington down the road, pelting him with anything they could lay their hands on.

Reactions like this seem extreme to us, but even today it's not unheard of for fights to break out at sports events when a fan is caught in the wrong hat in the wrong section of the stadium at the wrong time. These kinds of responses are a holdover from the days when hats carried a great deal of symbolic power. Just one glance at a person's head covering could tell you his or her religious beliefs, occupation, station in life, or marital status. Even how and when the hat was worn could speak volumes about the wearer.

The arrival of the closed automobile was the beginning of the end for the hat in our society. With the obvious exception of baseball caps and head coverings worn to protect us from the sun's harmful rays, people rarely don hats any more. They, like gloves, are artifacts of another era, symbols of an age when society was certainly more class-conscious but may also have been just a little bit more polite.

Painted Ladies and Tattooed Men

On September 19, 1991, two hikers high up in the Alps, on the border between Austria and Italy, stumbled upon the body of a man – another hiker, they assumed, who had fallen or lost his bearings in a sudden storm and died. They were right in a way, except that this "hiker" turned out to be more than five thousand years old.

Ötzi the Iceman was found with only his head and shoulders sticking out of the melting ice and snow in a remote mountain pass in the Ötztal region (from which he takes his name). Thinking he was a modern man who had been there for no more than a few years, the hikers called the police and the alpine rescue service, who proceeded to free Ötzi from his icy grave with the help of jackhammers and shovels. It wasn't until an archeologist saw the Iceman's copper ax that people began to understand the importance of this find: Ötzi is the oldest, best-preserved human specimen ever discovered.

The freezing temperatures of the ice had kept intact all of Ötzi's clothes – his shoes, his leather leggings and belt, his woven grass cloak – as well as his tools and weapons. And the ice had also preserved Ötzi himself, so much so that scientists say he looks as if he's been dead for only a few weeks. Examinations of his body have revealed that he was shot in the back with an arrow, that he ate unleavened bread and meat for his last meal, and that he was covered with tattoos on his spine, knees, and ankles. All this information has helped scientists in their quest to discover whether Ötzi died as the result of an accident, was murdered, or was the victim of a ritual sacrifice.

Tattoo You

Tattooing is one of the oldest forms of body art. People have been doing it since at least 8000 B.C., so it was not a great surprise that Ötzi was decorated in this way. But scientists couldn't agree on what his tattoos – more than fifty different lines and crosses –

meant. Were they tribal markings, proof that he belonged to one group of people and not another? Did they have religious significance and were perhaps evidence that he was killed as part of a ceremonial ritual? Or, the most intriguing possibility of all, were they the marks of an ancient acupuncture treatment for arthritis, a practice scientists had thought originated in China only two or three thousand years ago?

For now, the debate over the significance of Ötzi's tattoos rages on. But the different theories do highlight some of the many reasons people choose – or are forced – to mark themselves in this way. Tattoos are probably most commonly used to celebrate a rite of passage – from childhood to adulthood, for example. But they can also be a sign of membership in a group or a symbol of social undesirability. A tattoo can express religious beliefs, patriotic feelings, or love and devotion. It may even have medicinal significance or be viewed as a mark of beauty.

The first tattoo in literature is the mark that God gives Cain after he murders his brother, Abel, in the Book of Genesis. That tattoo was actually meant to protect Cain, who for his crime was condemned to wander in exile for the rest of his days. God wanted to be sure that no one who came upon Cain would be tempted to take revenge on him, so He marked him to show that he was the recipient of divine mercy. And just in case there was any confusion, He also commanded, "If any one slays Cain, vengeance shall be taken on him sevenfold."

But even for God, things don't always go according to plan. Very quickly, Cain's tattoo became a badge of shame, something that identified him and his crime to all he met, and ever since then, these so-called marks of Cain have been used to designate all types of social outcasts, from criminals and political prisoners to slaves, prostitutes, and other people on the fringes of society.

We know they used tattoos this way in the ancient world. Greeks and Romans marked their slaves and prisoners of war much as a modern-day rancher or farmer will use brands or ear tags to identify his cattle. In Greek, these tattoos were called *stigmatias*, which gives us the modern English word "stigma," meaning shame or disgrace.

Sometimes Roman slaves were tattooed with the letter *F*, for "fugitive,"

or even with the phrase "Stop me, I'm a runaway." There was certainly no chance that anyone marked this way could escape and blend in with free citizens. These *stigmatias* were also used on criminals, who sometimes were forced to have their crimes tattooed across their foreheads. This same custom was also practiced in many indigenous (Native) societies. The Mayan people of Central America, for instance, used facial tattoos to identify thieves.

In New Zealand, the Maori engaged in a type of facial tattooing called *moko* (literally "carving of the face"), but in this case, the tattoos were a symbol of pride, not shame. Maori men got their *moko* to frighten the enemy in battle and to prove their courage (facial tattoos are among the most painful you can get). These tattoos had the added benefit of being attractive to women; men who had no *moko* were called *papatea*, "plain face," and were widely scorned.

Indigenous peoples the world over seem to have practiced tattooing of one form or another. Incan mummies from the 1200s are proof of early tattooing in Peru, and we know from the accounts of European explorers that the practice was widespread among North

American Natives and the Inuit. In fact, carved figurines found in the Arctic confirm that facial tattooing among the Dorset peoples was common 3,500 years ago.

Different indigenous peoples used tattoos for different reasons. The Inuit, for example, often tattooed stick-like human figures that were called guardians and would protect the wearer from evil spirits, drowning, illness, and any other bad fortune. In Borneo, the Dyaks, some of the most tattooed people on earth, would decorate girls when they came of age and boys when they began to show success in hunting (especially, at one time, headhunting). Because the Dyaks believed that in the afterlife, everything is the reverse of how it is on earth, they liked their tattoos to be as dark as possible. In the gloom of the afterworld, the theory went, their black tattoos would gleam brightly, showing them the way to heaven.

In Japan, tattooing can be traced back to about 400 B.C. For some indigenous Japanese – like the Ainus, who may have been Japan's first inhabitants – tattooing was an important cultural ritual. Ainu women were much more likely than men to be tattooed,

and their markings were most often on the face. The tattoos were elaborate and would be completed over many years, starting when the girls were about ten and continuing until they were ready to marry. They symbolized goodness and purity, and thus were a sign the girl would make a good wife.

Perhaps because tattooing in Japan was so closely associated with Native peoples – who unfortunately were treated no better there than they often were in the rest of the world – the practice was not common elsewhere in the country. As in the ancient world, it was generally reserved for marking prisoners, a practice that dates back to at least the 1200s. In some parts of Japan, a wrongdoer's first crime would earn him one horizontal line. If he erred again, he'd get a small arch, and his third offense would merit a second horizontal line. Taken together, these three symbols formed the Japanese character for the word "dog," which pretty much sums up how the offender could expect to be treated once released.

So what was a man to do once he had been marked this way? Even those imprisoned for the most minor of crimes would have to display their guilt to the world for the rest of their lives.

In the days before laser surgery, when removing tattoos was not an option, the obvious answer was to cover them with other, more decorative markings. Soon, a new art form, called *irezumi* (literally, "insertion of ink"), emerged. Former printmakers from all over Japan found lucrative new careers concealing prison tattoos with traditional Japanese symbols like dragons and flowers.

For about a hundred years, from the mid-1700s to the mid-1800s, *irezumi* had a small but faithful following among not only former prisoners but also writers, artists, and other people who wanted to appear as if they were not part of mainstream society. When Japan began to open itself up to trade with the West in the 1850s, the craft gained new life among sailors from Britain and the United States, and then among upper-class tourists with a taste for adventure.

But even though Japanese tattooing had begun to make these inroads into so-called respectable society, it was still primarily used to identify criminals, a practice that eventually spread to most Western countries, including England, France, and the United States. The Roman practice of tattooing slaves

SCARRED FOR LIFE

For those rare souls who feel that puncturing the skin with a needle and infusing it with dyes and pigments is not extreme enough, there's always scarification to consider.

Used since ancient times to mark slaves so they couldn't run away or be taken by other slave owners, scarification was also popular among some early African tribes, such as the Yoruba and the Tiv, both of Nigeria. The bizarre practice involves cutting or burning the skin and rubbing in irritants such as ashes or ground charcoal to produce a permanent scar. It was a preferred form of body-marking for many Africans, whose darker skin made tattooing a less desirable option.

Like tattooing, voluntary scarification was used primarily to celebrate a rite of passage or to identify a person's rank within a tribe. Some believed scarification was a way to heal the sick, much as Europeans once believed in bloodletting. Many women even thought these marks made them more attractive to men, and so they often agreed to have their faces scarred. Like the stretched lips and elongated necks of the Mursi and Padaung women, these facial scars came to be considered a symbol of great beauty.

with single letters was put to use on English wrongdoers as well. Paupers or escaped slaves might be branded with a *V*, for "vagabond," while those who just generally behaved badly got an *M*, for "malefactor." In the American colonies, people could be tattooed for "crimes" as minor as blasphemy (cursing), drunkenness, and adultery.

If you think this happened only in less enlightened times, think again. The English didn't do away with penal tattooing until the mid-1800s. In fact, the practice was in use in some countries in the twentieth century – most infamously in Nazi Germany, where concentration camp inmates were tattooed with numbers on their left forearms. The Nazis also adopted the related custom of labeling people's clothes with symbols of their supposed crimes. The yellow stars of the Jews were one example; others included pink triangles for homosexuals and red triangles for political prisoners.

In some countries, convicts eventually began to tattoo each other. In an odd way, this was probably an attempt to regain some control, to turn the tables on those punishing them. Prisoners in the Soviet Union's notorious Gulag system, which housed political detainees for almost sixty years during the twentieth century, reportedly tattooed each other with letters meaning "prisoner of Brezhnev," the Soviet leader at the time, to stress that they were being held not because they had committed any crimes but only because he wanted them held.

Later, Gulag inmates developed a complex visual language of tattoos. Convicts had to earn the right to wear certain markings, and for those who understood the elaborate symbolism involved, one look could tell an inmate's number and type of convictions and his rank among other prisoners. In the new Russia, organized crime is rampant and inmates are more likely to bribe their way to the top of the heap. The skulls and pirate tattoos of old have been replaced by American-style dollar bills and pop icons.

Today tattoos are almost mainstream. They are so popular with rock stars, actors, and sports heroes, for instance, that you might almost imagine everybody has one. Most people who acquire tattoos do so to mark life's milestones – a special birthday, a graduation – but they are also used to summon good fortune and scare off bad, to attract the attention of the opposite sex, or as a symbol of faith or religious devotion. Nevertheless, for many people – especially nervous parents who fear a tattoo is the first sign of trouble in a teenage child – they remain forever linked with the seedy, lawless side of life.

Skin Deep

Tattooing is a form of what is called body modification. This term also applies to things like piercings, plastic surgery, foot-binding, and even the wearing of corsets. A more subtle – and considerably less painful – type of body modification is body-painting, an ancient art that dates back possibly hundreds of thousands of years.

People probably first painted their bodies using mud, which not only could be manipulated into decorative patterns but also was cooling and kept away pesky insects. As they became slightly more sophisticated, prehistoric people began using mineral pigments to coat their skin. Initially, these were probably also put to practical use. Red ochre could clean wounds, protect sensitive skin from sun and wind, and keep the body warm when temperatures dipped. Like mud, it also provided a measure of resistance to insects; the Walbiri, Aborigines of central Australia, still use red ochre to ward off flies.

Some ancient people used body-painting to connect with the spirit world or to attract the protective influence of guardian spirits. This may also be why body-painting was so often connected with rituals surrounding death. In many indigenous societies, sick people would be painted or rubbed with mineral pigments, either to summon the supernatural to make them well or to ensure they would have a guardian spirit along for the ride as they passed into the afterworld. The commonly used red and yellow ochres had the added benefit of preserving the body after death.

Early people had a vast array of paint colors to choose from. Yellows and reds were the most prevalent, but whites, browns, purples, and blues were also common. Different colors could represent different things; yellow ochre, for instance, was associated with the sun and so was thought to increase strength, while chalk and powdered limestone would turn the skin white like bleached bones to

frighten enemy tribesmen.

The idea of using body paint as a scare tactic gained favor as the centuries passed. Many warlike tribes of ancient Europe – including the Picts (whose name comes from the Latin word for "paint") of what is now northern Scotland, the Visigoths and the Saxons of Germany, and the Gauls of France – decorated themselves both to terrify their enemy in battle and to stir up their own passions before the fighting began. Prior to any clash, the Visigoths and the Saxons both dyed their hair (red and blue, respectively) to frighten their opponents into what they hoped would be early submission. The Gauls apparently took this custom one step further, bounding into battle not only with dyed blue hair and mustaches but also as naked as the day is long.

We know the Scots were still painting their bodies right into the 1200s. The great Scottish hero William Wallace (think *Braveheart*) commanded his followers to dye their skin blue with woad. Wallace understood that the ritual of painting themselves made his men feel more a part of the group, and therefore more likely to fight hard and even die for their cause; the severe

blue warpaint had the added bonus of giving them a terrible, intimidating appearance. Today we still practice a version of this warlike custom when we decorate our bodies and faces to urge on our favorite hockey or football team at the local arena.

Eventually, people began painting their bodies for purely aesthetic reasons. Patterns were striking and elaborate, and emphasized the natural strength and beauty of the human body. Even today, this is still the case. The Nuba of Sudan, for example, paint themselves with designs that, while beautiful, are not pictorial and don't necessarily relate to coming-of-age ceremonies or any other cultural rituals.

Of course, it isn't only tribal peoples who continue to practice the ancient art of body-painting. Even in the big cities of the Western world, we are really doing just that every time we put on lipstick or add a little color to our cheeks with blush. To conceal those little imperfections or enhance the features

THE ANCIENT ART OF MEHNDI

Perhaps the oldest continuously used makeup is henna, a reddish-orange dye that comes from the leaves of a small shrub. Women throughout the world, but especially in the Middle East and North Africa, have used henna for thousands of years. Some believe that people in what is now Turkey were adorning their hands with the dye as early as 7000 B.C.

The art of staining the body with henna is called mehndi. The earliest known written references to mehndi describe decorating the hands and feet for a wedding ceremony, and while the custom is also used to celebrate special events like engagements or pregnancies, it is still most often associated with weddings today.

In many parts of the world, the bride and her friends and family will have a "Night of the Henna" party before the wedding. Everyone joins together in ornamenting the bride and helping her prepare for the transition to adulthood. There is even a widely held belief that the deeper the stain the henna leaves on the bride's hands and feet, the longer the love between the bride and groom will last.

we admire, nothing works better than makeup, the most enduring type of body paint we have.

Not Just a Pretty Face

The modern cosmetics industry owes a huge debt of gratitude to the ancient Egyptians, who never went in for full body-painting, preferring instead to decorate themselves more modestly with eyeliner and even nail polish. They were the first to wear what we would think of as makeup, and they did it as early as 4000 B.C.

The Egyptians liked makeup primarily because they thought it made them look better, though some cosmetics probably had religious associations, and eye makeup was certainly used to cut the glare from the sun. At different stages of the empire's history, certain types of makeup were reserved for royal or high-born Egyptians, but over time, most trickled down to the common people. Men and even children donned at least eye makeup and sometimes also face powder and blush.

Egyptian women wore the most

makeup, of course – everything from eye shadow to lipstick to perfumes and lotions. They probably put up with a lot for beauty. Most makeup today is made from harmless substances like talc, oils, waxes, and colored pigments. But it wasn't this way for the Egyptians. They cleaned their teeth with abrasives, outlined their eyes with soot and ground ants' eggs, and ground up harsh minerals to make eyeshadow. Worst of all, they painted their faces with a white powder that was made with lead carbonate, a potential killer.

But the Egyptians weren't the only ones to suffer for the cause of beauty. In ancient India, women colored their eyelids with poisonous antimony, and the Romans used the same lead-based whitening face powder that was so toxic for the Egyptians. Even as we entered the Christian era, things didn't much improve. In the sixteenth and seventeenth centuries, women wore lipstick made from poisonous mercury and used hair bleach that contained sulfuric acid. One popular skin whitener, Venetian ceruse, was made of lead (just like in the ancient world), which could seep into the bloodstream, causing baldness and, eventually, death. And the Victorians were no

smarter. Women in the 1800s put toxic belladonna, also called deadly nightshade, into their eyes to make them shine, and they even sipped arsenic, a dangerous poison, to keep their skin looking young.

As strange as these ingredients often were, stranger still were some of the physical features once considered beautiful. Egyptian women admired varicose veins and would outline them with blue dye to really make them pop.

In the thirteenth century, dark-skinned Moors of Spain would bleed themselves to lighten their complexion and make their own blue veins stand out (a fruitless attempt to convince the judges of the Spanish Inquisition that their skin was white and their blood was pure). The Mayans of Central America, meanwhile, envied women lucky enough to have been born with crossed eyes. And if that wasn't odd enough, from the tenth century to the nineteenth, Japanese wives used a paste made of iron scraps soaked in tea to give their teeth the black appearance that was so admired at the time.

Today we are much too sophisticated to fall prey to all these foolish fads, right? Instead, we just go in for things like micropigmentation, which is essentially a way of permanently tattooing the face with eyeliner, lipstick, eyebrow pencil, and lip liner. Even more extreme, people have been known to inject their foreheads with small doses of the toxin that causes botulism, a kind of food poisoning, to rid themselves of those tell-tale lines and wrinkles. For persistent but minor facial scars and imperfections, women and men turn to deep chemical peels or, better yet, dermabrasion, which is sort of like going at the skin with sandpaper.

And all this isn't even to mention lip augmentation, chin and cheek implants, and something called blepharoplasty, which will cure the truly vain of those nagging dark circles under the eyes.

Anthropologists have called the human body the first canvas for artistic expression, and it seems we have been honing our skills since the Stone Age. We use our own skin to transmit messages about our social ranking, our marital status, our religious beliefs, even our concepts of beauty. Whether it's as simple as a dab of lipstick or as complex as a full-body tattoo, our impulse to decorate our own bodies is one of the customs that links us to the earliest members of the human family.

Put Your Best Foot Forward

We all know about the handsome prince who falls in love with a poor but beautiful stranger and has only a tiny, delicate slipper by which to identify her. This is the story of Cinderella, right? Well, yes. But it's also the story of Abadeha, in the Philippines; Aschenputtel, in Germany; Yen-Hsien, in China; Sootface, among the Ojibwa peoples; and Vasilissa, in Russia. In fact, hundreds of variations of this same story can be found all over the world, going back many, many centuries. In what is perhaps the most familiar version, Cinderella's special shoe is made of glass, but in others, it's made of gold, silver, or even fur. Sometimes Cinderella loses her shoe in her rush to get home before midnight, and sometimes the shoe comes off when it sticks to tar the prince has spread all over his palace steps. Even the stepsisters differ from story to story. Usually they are unkind yet redeemable, but in several versions they are pure evil.

HERE COMES THE BRIDE

It's no accident that shoes crop up in so many of our most enduring stories and fairy tales — not only in the Cinderella story but also in *Puss in Boots*, *The Shoemaker and the Elves*, *The Twelve Dancing Princesses*, and *The Wizard of Oz*. Shoes have a mythical, magical quality — we associate them with good luck, prosperity, even fertility.

Perhaps this is why shoes also play a role in marriage rituals in countless cultures and countries. At one time it was common for a member of the bride's family, usually her father or mother, to give a pair of her shoes to the groom during a wedding ceremony to symbolize that she had become his responsibility. Traces of this custom still remain in our modern habit of tying shoes and boots to the bumper of the newlyweds' honeymoon car.

And they don't always just try to squeeze their unattractively large feet into the dainty shoe; in the gory 1812 story by the Brothers Grimm, the sisters actually attempt to change the size of their feet by cutting off toes and even their heels.

Why have these stories appeared in country after country, across miles and through centuries? And what do they all mean? All we really know for sure is that they were passed down orally from one generation to the next, and that they traveled between cultures that had long-standing connections to one another. Some people suspect that Cinderella's transformation from raggedy housemaid to beautiful princess is really a way of explaining the setting and rising of the sun or the change of seasons from winter to spring. Others have suggested that the story is a way of describing an actual event known as the imperial brideshow. In this ancient custom, popular at one time in places such as Russia and China, eligible girls would be paraded in front of a king or emperor who was seeking a bride. They would be examined from head to toe, with special attention paid to the foot. Those whose feet were small and dainty — like Cinderella's — were especially prized.

Small is Beautiful

Small, delicate feet have been a hallmark of beauty for women probably for thousands – possibly hundreds of thousands – of years. Foot size is such a strong indicator of attractiveness, in fact, that women have sometimes gone to extreme and painful lengths to make their feet appear smaller. The most drastic example of this is the practice of foot-binding, popular in China for many centuries. Some people suggest that this custom is the true origin of the Cinderella story.

No one knows exactly when or why foot-binding first began to be practiced in China. One common theory is that it had something to do with Empress Taki, who was born in the eleventh century with club feet (when the foot is turned down and in, so the person can walk only on the outer edge). Her father, to spare her embarrassment as she got older, supposedly decreed that all high-born women would mimic the shape of the empress's feet, and so they began to bind and deform their own. Another theory also focuses on the father of Empress Taki. This one suggests that he had court dancers who were celebrated for their tiny feet, and who even wrapped them in strips of cloth as a kind of forerunner to today's ballet shoe. The women would dance on a floor covered with blossoms from

the lotus flower, a symbol of beauty, purity, and grace. These dancers were so admired that Chinese women everywhere began binding their own feet to imitate them. Soon the tiny shoes they wore to give their feet some small measure of protection became known as lotus shoes.

Whatever its origins, foot-binding was a brutal custom. Mothers would start the process when their daughters were between five and seven, and their bones were still able to be molded into shape. Using strips of cloth as much as ten feet (3 meters) long, the women would tightly wrap the children's feet, bending the four smaller toes underneath and toward the heel. It was an agonizingly slow and painful procedure. Over a period of anywhere from two to six years, the process was repeated again and again, with the feet more and more tightly bound each time. Eventually, the bones of the feet would actually break and be forced up, giving the appearance of a tiny foot with a high arch. The ideal was a foot that could fit a shoe only three inches (7.5 centimeters) long and as little as two inches (5 centimeters) wide, the so-called golden lotus.

With their feet so utterly deformed,

the girls were generally unable to walk without help. This was the point of the exercise, to a large degree: families who bound their daughters' feet were showing they were wealthy enough to support members who would never hold jobs of their own. Most girls whose feet had been bound led inactive lives waiting for men to select them as brides. The smaller a girl's feet, the greater her chances of marrying into an established, high-class Chinese family. While the girls waited, their mothers taught them how to care for their feet; the bindings were tight, airless, and rarely removed, so women had to fight a constant, lifetime battle against odor and infection. They also learned to make the lotus shoes, those exquisitely embroidered, hand-stitched slippers that hid their highly desirable tiny feet from men's lustful eyes. Learning to create these shoes was as important a cultural activity as the foot-binding itself.

Over time, this custom became extremely popular and spread to most levels of Chinese society in many regions of the country. At its peak, more than 40 percent of Chinese women had bound feet. And though we may think of it as typical of ancient, less enlightened times, foot-binding was common well into the twentieth century. The practice was officially banned in China in 1912, but it lingered on in remote communities far beyond that. The last factory to make lotus shoes as part of its regular line stopped producing them in 1998!

The Height of Fashion

The Chinese are certainly not the only people who ever chose beauty over comfort, as we have seen. For centuries people the world over have been following trends and falling victim to customs that may seem ridiculous to us today. In fact, we have, in the modern high heel shoe, the remnants of one of the most absurd of all fashion fads.

High heels began to appear in France in the late 1500s. Surprisingly, men were the first to wear them, and this is perhaps because they realized that a raised heel had a practical application: it helped them keep their feet in the stirrups when they were riding. And the high heel served other purposes as well. For those who lived in cities like Paris and London, it was the

THE FIRST SHOES

The first shoes — apart from those made simply by tying strips of bark or fur to the foot — were probably sandals. We know that Egyptians were wearing sandals as early as 3700 B.C., and the Greeks and Romans wore them as well.

In societies where the style of dress was quite simple, the sandal became a place to display wealth and social status. In ancient Rome, high-born citizens regularly decorated their sandals with gold and small gems. Sometimes even the soles of the shoes got special attention. Ancient Egyptians, for example, would paint a likeness of their enemies there so they could tramp on them with every step.

Religious leaders often wore simple sandals — or even went barefoot — as evidence of their indifference to every-day luxuries. This was also a way of expressing some unity with slaves and members of the poorer classes, who could rarely afford shoes and usually went without. This custom has even carried over to modern times. In one of the most famous protests of the twentieth century, Mahatma Gandhi marched 230 miles (370 kilometers) across India to defy British taxation laws in a handwoven loincloth and a simple pair of leather sandals.

perfect solution to the problem of hopelessly muddy and waste-filled streets because it kept the feet raised a few inches off the ground. For men of influence who happened to have been born a little on the short side, the heels also offered an opportunity to increase stature. It is said that France's Louis XIV, who was less than five-foot-six (168 centimeters), seemed much more powerful and imposing when he put on his standard five-inch (12 centimeter) heels.

But women quickly took to this new style of footwear too, and most men were glad of it; women in high heels – even today – somehow seem more fragile, more in need of assistance, than women in flat, "sensible" shoes. Although the extra few inches of height they gain gives them more confidence, that is offset by their hobbled walk and the actual physical distortion of the foot. In fact, the high heel is not that far removed from the Chinese lotus shoe; the goal of both was to manipulate the foot until it appeared smaller and more delicate. By pushing the back of the foot up at an awkward and unnatural angle and forcing the wearer to support all her weight up front, the high heel tricks the eye into

seeing a longer leg and a smaller foot. And like lotus shoes, high heels originally signaled that their wearer had no desire or need to earn her own living. If you had a physically demanding job – or simply wanted to move around quickly and in comfort – the high heel was not for you.

High heels for women may have had their origins in sixteenth-century Venice, home to the chopine, without a doubt the silliest type of footwear ever created. The chopine was something like a mini pedestal that sloped forward at the front of the foot. Venetian women must have been gluttons for punishment: their chopines routinely reached twenty inches (50 centimeters) in height or more. These towering platforms were so impossible to walk in that women had to turn to their ever-present servants for help. Tottering about like circus performers on stilts, they thought they were the very height of fashion.

Some people today believe that the chopines, as ridiculous as they seem to us, did serve a practical purpose: women who might otherwise have been tempted to stray from their husbands couldn't get around easily enough to have affairs. There is some evidence to support this theory. Although the Church commonly waded into the fashion arena, restricting various articles of clothing through those pesky sumptuary laws, it never had a word to say about chopines.

Not surprisingly, the chopine never really caught on outside Venice. It did have a more practical cousin, however, in the patten, popular especially in England and France from at least the 1300s into the nineteenth century. The purpose of the patten, like heels in general, was to raise the foot up to protect it from the muddy, unpaved streets that were everywhere in Europe before the late 1700s. Pattens took many forms. Some were iron rings that strapped on to existing shoes (similar to the blades that some children wear strapped to their boots when they're learning to skate). Others were a kind of clog, with thick soles made of wood or sometimes cork.

The patten was such a sensible shoe that its counterparts – like the Turkish *takunya* and the Dutch clog – can be found in cultures the world over. In Japan, both women and men wore wooden-soled shoes called *geta*. These usually had two slats, or risers, one in front and one in back. The risers could be the same height or differing heights, depending on the purpose of the shoe. Sushi chefs reportedly wore *geta* that were as much as twelve inches (30 centimeters) high so they could stand

comfortably at the raised counters common in sushi bars. Courtesans and geishas also favored *geta*. In their case, the ordinarily plain wooden slats would often be highly decorated and could challenge the height of some Venetian chopines. These women would need attendants to help them walk.

If you're thinking men are somehow immune to the whims of footwear fashion, think again. They can be just as devoted to foolish fads as women – witness the poulaine. This shoe, popular in Europe first in the twelfth century and again in the fifteenth, featured a long, curving toe that would often be stuffed with horsehair to hold its shape. All men of taste wore them, driving the fashion to more and more ludicrous levels. Eventually, the toe

points were so long that they had to be fastened by thin chains to the knee or even the waist to allow men to walk. They were such a symbol of social status that ultimately the length of the toe had to be regulated by law, with one size for royalty and another for lesser men. No one wanted a "commoner" mascarading as something more by striding about in shoes he was not legally entitled to wear.

The Modern Shoe

Amazingly enough, several of these bizarre shoe styles do have modern counterparts. We can see, for instance, the influence of the chopine in the platform sneakers and boots that are

popular with many teenagers today. The poulaine had a brief resurgence in the 1950s, in a shoe called the winkle-picker, which was favored by a group of working-class English trend-setters known as the Teddy Boys. And even clogs made a strong comeback among hippies in the 1960s.

But far and away the most popular shoe today is the running shoe, or sneaker. While we may think of this as a thoroughly modern shoe style, however, the sneaker has actually been around since the mid-1800s, when a rubber-soled shoe with a canvas top was first introduced for players of croquet and then tennis. In the early 1900s, this canvas shoe became popular for children, perhaps because it was comfortable, easy to walk in, and durable. And by the 1950s, this non-mainstream shoe had been taken up by rebellious teenagers who had no desire to look, act, or – especially – dress like their parents.

But canvas shoes with rubber soles were still primarily sold as athletic shoes, and as sports of all kinds – basketball, baseball, track events – grew in popularity, there was more and more demand for lightweight, long-lasting footwear. With the arrival of television

THE COBBLER'S DEMISE

For thousands of years, people went to shoemakers, or cobblers, to have all their footwear made by hand. A cobbler would measure each customer's feet and assemble shoes and boots specifically for that person. It was a time-consuming but ancient craft, and like many ancient activities, it is shrouded in myth and legend. One of the most gruesome centers on Hugh of Wales, a shoemaker who was put to death for his religious beliefs in about 300 A.D. According to legend, Hugh's fellow cobblers stole his body off the gibbet (where dead criminals were hung as a warning to others), dried his bones, and turned them into shoemaking tools. Ever since then, the shoemaker's toolkit has been known as St. Hugh's bones.

Starting in the 1800s, the Industrial Revolution radically changed the production of footwear. Machines were invented that could sew shoes at speeds cobblers couldn't dream of, and a wide variety of footwear suddenly became available to the great mass of people. Shoemakers started to carry lines of shoes in several different sizes. People could buy them on the spot, choosing whichever size fit them best. Gone forever was the craft of the cobbler – and with it went the days when a person's footwear told you everything about him.

STEPPING OUTSIDE THE LAW

Would you believe that a simple foot-print can help solve a crime? It's true. In recent years, crime scene analysts have begun to realize the value of footwear evidence in a criminal investigation. In fact, many forensic scientists now believe this evidence is more reliable than fingerprints in identifying suspects.

Shoeprints, unlike fingerprints, can reveal a variety of useful information. Some simple calculations will result in a suspect's shoe size, weight, and approximate height. Footprints can also show the path into and away from a crime scene, the number of suspects, and where and in what order events took place during the crime.

Perhaps most important, foot-prints can tell crime scene investigators the make and model of the shoe the perpetrator wore. With running shoes, this is especially true, since the hyper-competitive shoe manufacturers are constantly releasing new models, each with a sole pattern unlike that of any other shoe. By looking at that sole pattern, investigators can easily isolate the type of shoe worn. In some cases, this can lead to a list of customers who bought that model in local stores, vastly reducing the pool of potential suspects.

in the mid-twentieth century, sports took another leap forward. Individual athletes soon became heroes of popular culture, just like singers and film stars, and companies realized the value of marketing the shoes they wore to the general public. And if you want to sell the products that athletes wear, what better pitchmen could there be than the athletes themselves?

Today we are used to seeing sports heroes of all kinds – soccer players, tennis stars, famous runners and golfers – endorse product lines for shoe companies, but it's really a relatively new phenomenon. One of the first – and most successful – partnerships between a shoe manufacturer and a sports superstar was the one involving Nike and Michael Jordan. In 1985, his rookie year in the NBA, Jordan helped design and promote the first Air Jordans. These black, white, and red high-topped shoes were actually not allowed in the NBA (black would mark the courts), but Jordan wore them anyway, racking up fines every time he played.

Among basketball fans, particularly inner-city teens and pre-teens, there was soon a mania for these shoes. No kid could hope to be viewed as hip and cool unless he had a pair. But at more than a

hundred dollars a pop, they were often beyond the means of most parents. And as a result, the shoes soon sparked a new trend: kids committing violent muggings and even murders to take by force what they couldn't afford any other way. Never wanting to miss an opportunity, the shoe companies started releasing new models each year – just as automobile companies do with cars and trucks – to fuel the hysteria. Today the shelf life of the average running shoe is about two months.

Whether it's brawling in the streets or hobbling about on ultra-high heels, shoes seem to have the power to make us want to do crazy things. In fact, they inspire in us a passion no other clothing can. Perhaps this is because they say so much about who we are – even in these days of mass production. We choose different shoes for different occasions, use them to make political statements, even modify our taste in them as we progress through life. They are our most personal item of clothing, actually conforming to the shape of our feet over time, as if they had been made just for us.

All the things we wear – from head to toe – have at times in the past marked our class, betrayed our humble origins, or prevented us from enjoying everything society had to offer. But they also have the power to lift us up, to give us confidence, to make us feel better about ourselves with every step we take.

Notes

There are many good books of general fashion history and the history of specific items of clothing. These notes acknowledge the sources I relied on most heavily.

Chapter 1: Girl Power

Amelia Bloomer's life has been well documented. For a good, basic introduction to her life and accomplishments, visit the website for the American Experience television series at www.pbs.org/wgbh/amex/eleanor/sfeature/fashion_1.html. The quotation from Elizabeth Smith Miller is taken from an article in the collection of the New York Public Library. Some of the information on hoop skirts is drawn from a website that focuses on period costume; it can be accessed at www.corsetsandcrinolines.com. The stories of the Portuguese queen and the production of Handel's *Messiah* are drawn from *Let There Be Clothes* by Lynn Schnurnberger (New York: Workman Publishing, 1991). The interview with Mary Quant appeared in the October 10, 1967, issue of the British newspaper the *Guardian*. Some of the information about stockings and, later, about swimsuits and bathing machines is drawn from *The Way We Are* by Margaret Visser (Toronto: HarperCollins, 1994), a book that, in many ways, was the model for this one. The item about hip-hugging jeans appeared in the January 9, 2003, issue of the *Toronto Star*. The information about corsets is drawn, in large part, from *The Corset: A Cultural History* by Valerie Steele (New Haven, CN: Yale University Press, 2001). The stories about making corsets into battleships and barring schoolgirls from wearing them are from *Let There Be Clothes*. The quip from Louis Reard can be found in countless books and on numerous websites.

Chapter 2: Clothes Make the Man

For a good overview of the Zoot Suit Riots, see the American Experience website at www.pbs.org/wgbh/amex/zoot/index.html. Much of the information about Levi Strauss and early blue jeans is drawn from the Levi Strauss & Co. corporate website at www.levistrauss.com/about/history. For information about vintage and "new vintage" jeans, I am indebted to an article by Austin Bunn in the December 1, 2002, issue of the *New York Times Magazine*. The history of men's neckwear is drawn, in large part, from *The Tie: Trends and Traditions* by Sarah Gibbings (Hauppauge, NY: Barron's, 1991). Some of the information about handkerchiefs, particularly the signals that could be sent with them, can also be found in *Hanky Panky* by Helen Gustafson (Berkeley, CA: Ten Speed Press, 2002). The story about using hankies as dog tags comes from the *World Book Encyclopedia*. Some information about the history of eyeglasses is drawn from an article by Dr. Richard D. Drewry; it can be accessed at www.eye.utmem.edu/history/glass.html. The remark about "reading through the rips" was made by Margaret Visser in *The Way We Are*.

Chapter 3: Topping It All Off

The story about the battles between the clergy and the nobility regarding hair length is drawn from *Extraordinary Popular Delusions and the Madness of Crowds* by Charles Mackay (1852; reprint New York: Harmony Books, 1980). The Egyptian cures for baldness are described in an article by Roberta Shaw in the Summer 1999 issue of *Rotunda* (the magazine of the Royal Ontario Museum). The stories about Babylonians sprinkling their locks with gold dust and fifteenth-century women plucking the hair at their hairlines are mentioned in *Let There Be Clothes*. Some of the information about wigs is drawn from *The Way We Are*. The fashion for blond-colored wigs in ancient Rome is mentioned in *Let There Be Clothes*, which is also the source for the rumor about wigs being made from the hair of plague victims. The comment about the wig-wearing conspiracy was made by Margaret Visser in *The Way We Are*. The

description of wig-making is drawn from several websites, including one maintained by the wigmaker of Sweden's Gothenburg Opera, which can be accessed at www.makeup-fx.com/perukmakeri1eng.html. An item about the group called Lawyers Against Wigs appeared in the September 1, 1986, issue of *Time* magazine. Much of the information about the sometimes perplexing shaving habits of men is drawn from *One Thousand Beards* by Alan Peterkin (Vancouver: Arsenal Pulp Press, 2001).

Chapter 4: Accessories After the Fact
Information about the jewelry preferences of the Egyptians is drawn from the *Rotunda* article by Roberta Shaw. The stories of restrictions being placed on certain metals in Roman times and of unmarried women being barred from wearing jewelry are mentioned in *Let There Be Clothes*. The neck-stretching practices of the Padaung women are well known; some information and photographs can be found at www.myanmar.com. The story of the ring worn by the pope is drawn from the *World Book Encyclopedia*. The Canadian "Ritual of the Calling of an Engineer" – which includes the ring ceremony – was conceived by Rudyard Kipling. Some of the information about gloves and the etiquette of wearing them is drawn from *The Way We Are*. The story of poor Jonas Hanway and his struggles to be accepted, umbrella and all, is widely known; his plight is recounted in both *The Way We Are* and *Let There Be Clothes*, and in many other places. Some of the information about the history of headwear is drawn from *Hats: Status, Style, and Glamour* by Colin McDowell (New York: Thames and Hudson, 1992). The meaning behind the words "falsehood" and "hoodwink" is described in *Let There Be Clothes*.

Chapter 5: Painted Ladies and Tattooed Men
There is no lack of information about Ötzi the Iceman. Some useful photos can be found on the websites of the Discovery Channel (at dsc.discovery.com/convergence/iceman/iceman.html) and the South Tyrol Museum of Archaeology (at www.archaeologiemuseum.it/f06_ice_uk.html), where he now "lives." For some additional information about Ötzi's tattoos, I am indebted to Melitta Franceschini, who works at the museum. Some of the details about tattooing and other forms of body art are drawn from an article titled "Body Art as Visual Language" by Enid Schildkrout in the Winter 2001 issue of *AnthroNotes*, a publication of the Museum of Natural History at the Smithsonian Institution. Mark Gustafson wrote a helpful scholarly article about prison and slave tattoos for the April 1997 issue of the journal *Classical Antiquity*. The story of the Japanese tattoo that spells out the word "dog" is mentioned in John Gray's *I Love Mom: An Irreverent History of the Tattoo* (Toronto: Key Porter, 1994); Gray also discusses the art of *irezumi*. Alix Lambert's documentary *The Mark of Cain* explores the world of tattooing in the Russian prison system. A good, brief article about body-painting as a primitive art form can be found in the *Cambridge Illustrated History of Prehistoric Art* by Paul G. Bahn (Cambridge: Cambridge University Press, 1998). Also useful is the book *Body Marks: Tattooing, Piercing, and Scarification* by Kathlyn Gay and Christine Whittington (Brookfield, CN: Millbrook Press, 2002).

Chapter 6: Put Your Best Foot Forward
Some of the information on foot-binding is drawn from an exhibition called "Every Step a Lotus: Shoes in the Lives of Women in Late Imperial China." The exhibition, mounted at Toronto's Bata Shoe Museum, was curated by Dorothy Ko. The book *Shoes: Fashion and Fantasy* by Colin McDowell (New York: Thames and Hudson, 1989) offers a concise overview of the history of high heels and, especially, chopines. This is also the source for the story about St. Hugh of Wales. That ancient Egyptians used to paint a likeness of their enemies of the soles of their sandals is mentioned in *Let There Be Clothes*. Some of the quips, particularly the one about Elizabeth I and that about the Dutch smuggler's clogs, are drawn from information gathered at the Bata Shoe Museum. The information about Michael Jordan and the mania for basketball shoes comes largely from my own memory, which alas reaches back to the mid-1980s and before.

index